The In-House Accelerator

About the Author: John Jenkins is Editor of DealLawyers.com, TheCorporateCounsel.net, CompensationStandards.com, and the Deal Lawyers print newsletter. He also is a partner in the Cleveland office of Calfee, Halter & Griswold LLP, where he advises clients on capital markets transactions and SEC compliance, mergers and acquisitions, and corporate matters. John also serves as a member of the firm's executive committee.

John frequently writes and speaks about corporate and securities law, and previously served as an adjunct faculty member at The Cleveland-Marshall College of Law, Cleveland State University, where he taught a course in mergers and acquisitions law for a decade.

Foreword: This book is just one of a package of publications relating to corporate governance, corporate disclosures & practices and M&A offered by the publisher. The author is part of the team that maintains the popular sites –TheCorporateCounsel.net, CompensationStandards.com, and DealLawyers.com. This edition includes reported developments through November 2017.

I want to thank Broc Romanek for editing duties (and inspiration), plus my colleague Liz Dunshee, who was an indispensable partner on the larger project of building out numerous podcasts for those new to being in-house.

For more extensive materials, each of these Treatises contain more than 1600 pages of practical guidance:

- Romanek's "In-House Essentials Treatise" - Hard copy of the definitive work for in-house securities lawyers
- Romanek's "Proxy Season Disclosure Treatise" - Hard copy of the definitive work on the proxy season
- Lynn, Borges & Romanek's "Executive Compensation Disclosure Treatise" - Online version of this Treatise is part of a CompensationStandards.com membership - but hard copies of the book can be purchased separately

Legal Disclaimer: This publication is designed to provide accurate and authoritative information in regard to the subject matter covered; it should not be relied upon as legal advice. It is sold with the understanding that

Published By: EP EXECUTIVE PRESS, INC.

P. O. Box 1549
Austin, TX 78767

info@thecorporatecounsel.net / **512.485.1288**

Table of Contents

A. Board Leadership

1. Are companies required to have independent board chairs?

No - independent board chairs aren't required by corporate law, SEC rules or exchange rules. In fact, it's not at all unusual for an insider (i.e. the CEO) to serve as the board chair. The annual "Spencer Stuart Board Index" continues to show that a majority of S&P 500 companies combine the chair and CEO positions (52% in 2016).

Instead of opting for an independent board chair, many companies name a lead director. As of 2017, this remains the most common form of independent board leadership: 87% of S&P 500 boards report having a lead or presiding director, nearly all of whom (98%) are identified by name in the proxy.

2. Are companies required to separate the CEO & Chair positions?

No, there's no requirement to separate the CEO & board chair positions. However, separation of these positions has become a cause celebre for some governance activists in recent years.

According to Spencer Stuart's 2016 Board Index, 27% of S&P 500 boards, versus 21% in 2011, have an independent chair. That's actually down a bit over 2015, but the trend over the past decade is toward more companies having an independent chair. The number of S&P 500 companies that were led by a dual chair/CEO dropped from 77% in 2001 to 71% in 2006.

The theory behind the idea of an independent chair is that it enhances board oversight of management. CalPERS (a big institutional investor) likes to analogize a combined chair/CEO as allowing a student to grade his or her own paper.

Separating the chair and CEO positions makes a clear divide between the role of the board and the role of management, and gives one director clear authority to speak on behalf of the board and to run board meetings.

Separating the two positions is supposed to eliminate conflicts in evaluating management performance, setting compensation, management succession planning, and in recruiting new directors.

Advocates believe that it also reduces distraction for the CEO – who can now focus exclusively on matters relating to the business, while the chair addresses management oversight, board leadership, and governance.

That's the theory, but the reality is that not everybody subscribes to it. Splitting the positions can be very artificial, especially if the company already has somebody in both roles. It can also lead to turf battles, create internal confusion about who's in charge, and impair decision-making. Sometimes it can make it harder to attract a new CEO, who may expect to hold both positions or feel undermined if the positions are separate.

3. **What are proxy advisor policies on separation of the CEO & Chair?**

Proxy advisors – ISS and Glass Lewis are the big ones in the US - like policies that call for a separate CEO and chair. With the notable exception of State Street (a big institutional investor), so do most major institutional investors.

Under its latest policy, ISS typically recommends voting for independent chair proposals, taking into consideration the following factors: (1) the scope of the proposal; (2) the company's current board leadership structure; (3) the company's governance structure and practices; (4) the company's performance; and (5) any other relevant factors that may be applicable.

They will sometimes opt not to support a proposal if the company has an independent lead director whose role is sufficiently strong.

For example, if the lead director has approval rights with respect to agenda and materials sent to directors for board meetings, approves meeting schedules, can call meetings, and is available to meet with major shareholders, then that may be enough to persuade ISS not to back a proposal for an independent lead director. But that's not a guarantee.

Glass Lewis takes the position that an independent chair is in the long-term best interests of shareholders and the company, and will typically support shareholder proposals that seek to separate the roles of CEO and chair.

4. **What disclosure obligations do companies have regarding board leadership?**

Under Item 407(h) of the SEC's Regulation S-K, companies' proxy statements must disclose their board's leadership structure and the reasons why the company believes the structure is appropriate. Specifically, companies must disclose:

- Whether - and why - the company has chosen to combine or separate the CEO and board chair positions
- If the positions are combined, whether the company has designated a lead independent director and the specific role the lead independent director plays in the leadership of the board

- The reasons why the company determined its board leadership structure to be appropriate at the time of the filing

These rules also require that companies disclose the extent of the board's role in risk oversight of the company - such as how the board administers its oversight function - and the effect that this has on the board's leadership structure.

NYSE-listed companies also have to disclose the name of the director who presides over their board's executive sessions of non-management and independent directors. If the presiding director position rotates, then the procedure by which the presiding director is selected must be disclosed.

The NYSE standards also require listed companies to disclose a method for shareholders and other interested parties to communicate directly with the presiding director or the non-management/independent directors as a group.

This information about the presiding director needs to be on the company's website - with a cross-reference in the proxy statement – or you can put the full disclosure in the proxy statement itself.

5. Do companies adopt formal policies on board leadership?

Most companies don't have a formal policy requiring the separation or combination of the CEO and chair roles.

Looking at the 100 largest companies as of 2015, of the 37 companies with separate CEOs and chairs, 19 have adopted an explicit policy of splitting or combining the two positions - with 11 companies opting for separation and 8 choosing combination.

According to Spencer Stuart's 2015 Board Index, only 21 boards, or 4%, have formal policies requiring the separation - although this represents a modest increase from 3% in 2014 and 1% in 2010. However, Wells Fargo (after a crisis in 2017) made a very high-profile decision to amend its bylaws to require an independent chair, so there have been some notable additions to the list of companies requiring such a policy.

B. Board Meetings

6. How often are board & committee meetings typically held?

In the ordinary course, most boards meet 4 to 6 times per year. However, some companies meet more frequently – for example, banks typically hold monthly board meetings. If there are significant developments in the business - such as M&A activity, regulatory issues or if the company is in financial difficulties - boards may meet much more frequently.

7. Who establishes the agenda for the meetings? What matters are typically covered?

The CEO and management may take the lead in putting the agenda together, but it is a joint effort with the board – particularly if there's an independent chair.

In the absence of an independent chair, there's typically a lead or presiding director who will review and provide input into the board agenda, and there is also typically input from other directors about what goes on the agenda.

This, by the way, is a big deal to institutional investors – they don't want management to control what the board addresses. They want active board involvement and authority to set the agenda.

In terms of what goes on the agenda, there are a number of recurring items that are typically addressed. The prior board meeting minutes are reviewed and approved, there's a report from the CEO covering the business, operating results and projections. The CEO may be joined by other executives in making this report.

The CFO will address financial aspects of the company's operations – financial condition, liquidity, capital requirements and financing activity, etc. They'll be a report on legal and compliance issues. There may be reports from individual business units as well.

There will likely also be some input on investor relations (reports on conferences, analyst and investor meetings, etc.) The board will also receive reports from its standing committees – typically the audit committee, governance committee and compensation committee. And there will typically be an executive session where the board meets without any members of management present.

The board might also need to take action on specific items – and if that's the case, they'll be on the agenda. For example, the board may be considering and acting upon a proposed acquisition or divestiture, a financing, personnel matters, executive compensation arrangements, governance matters, or specific regulatory requirements that must be addressed in the course of the meeting.

8. What type of materials are typically provided to the directors in advance of the meeting?

The topics on the meeting agenda drive the materials included in the board package. So, board packages typically contain material that addresses the recurring matters that come up regularly at board meetings as well as materials relating to any unique items that warrant board review or approval.

For example, most board packages will include information detailing the company's performance versus projections, a review of operations, financial information, committee reports, minutes for the last meeting and an updated calendar of board and committee meetings.

Depending on the time of year, the board will also receive things like budget information, the company's strategic plan, earnings releases and SEC filings, draft 10-Ks and annual reports, proxy materials and related things like independence and audit committee expert determinations, and the annual self-evaluation materials.

In addition to these items, there may be materials relating to specific matters to be addressed by the board. These vary depending on the nature of the matter, but may include presentation materials relating to acquisitions, financings, legal or regulatory issues or governance topics. The board package typically also includes forms of proposed resolutions for any action that the board will take at the meeting.

The real challenge is keeping all this information manageable and digestible – and that's becoming more and more difficult as regulatory requirements and governance expectations continue to grow.

Before throwing anything and everything into the board package, it's important to think about whether your directors will actually be able to review the quantity and type of information that you're providing.

In my experience, directors aren't shy about telling you if you're drowning them in trivia, but you should talk with the board and make sure that the materials meet their needs and expectations.

9. Who typically attends the board & committee meetings?

The core players at board and committee meetings are the directors, the CEO & CFO, the General Counsel and the corporate secretary (if that's someone other than the General Counsel).

But frequently – based on the agenda – they may be joined by outside counsel, other members of management, the company's auditors, investment bankers and others who will address particular topics. It is customary in many situations for individuals to attend only the portion of the meeting to which they're relevant, and to be excused upon completion of their role.

10. Are there best practices when it comes to board minutes?

There are some best practices for board minutes. First of all, you want to make sure that all the procedural information about the meeting is appropriately documented: the date, time and place of the meeting, who was in attendance, whether it was conducted in person or by telephone, who chaired the meeting, who served as secretary and recorded the minutes, what topics were addressed, when it was adjourned, and any specific actions taken by the board (including resolutions that were adopted).

If legal advice is given, that fact should be noted and the fact that the discussion was privileged should be noted, but the advice itself should not be disclosed in the minutes – though it may make sense to memorialize it separately.

Lawyers have differing views on what comes next. Some advocate a "short form" approach, which doesn't provide any detail on director discussion, but just reflects the actions taken by the board. Others advocate a "long form" approach, where there's a detailed recitation of board discussion and debate on each topic addressed.

The best argument for short form minutes is that they are clear, concise and don't create the potential ambiguities that long-form minutes can create – and they're less likely to provide plaintiffs lawyers with an opportunity for extended frolics during depositions.

But, they also don't show the board's deliberation and the work and thought that went into a decision – and in many of the most important cases, the board may have to show this work in order to get the protection of the business judgment rule for its decisions.

Long form avoids this issue, but can create misconceptions about whether the board devoted sufficient attention to particular topics at a meeting and can create ambiguities that plaintiffs can seize on in litigation. Not for nothing, but they are also a pain in the neck to draft.

Many people opt for something in between, and use judgment concerning which board matters should be described in greater detail.

C. Board Committees & Responsibilities

11. Why do boards establish committees?

There are many reasons that boards might establish committees. Certain key committees are required by exchange rules, while others may be used to address conflicts of interest, oversee acquisitions, address derivative claims, conduct investigations, or otherwise perform work that the full board deems appropriate to delegate.

Committees can help protect the full board - particularly in situations where a majority of the directors are not disinterested. Under most corporate statutes, in discharging their fiduciary duties, directors are allowed to rely in good faith upon actions of committees on which they do not serve, if the actions are within the committee's authority.

12. What committees are companies required to have?

Under NYSE rules, listed companies must have the three key committees: an audit committee, a compensation committee and a governance/nominating committee. Although Nasdaq doesn't require a separate governance/nominating committee, director nominees must be selected either by an independent nominating committee or independent directors constituting a majority of the board's independent directors in a vote in which only independent directors participate.

Nearly all Nasdaq companies establish a separate governance/nominating committee, since it's viewed as a best practice and makes it easier to address nominating and governance responsibilities.

13. What are the requirements for serving on standing committees?

Audit, compensation and nominating/governance committees must consist solely of independent directors, with independence being established under exchange standards. Members of the audit committee and compensation committee have to satisfy heightened independence standards, and members of the audit committee also have to be financially sophisticated.

Not all working committees consist solely of independent directors – for example, many companies have an executive committee empowered to act for the board between meetings. The CEO and other insiders frequently serve on that committee.

14. Are committees required to have charters?

Charters aren't required as a matter of corporate law – a committee's authority can be described in a resolution or the bylaws - but most committees do. The NYSE requires the audit, compensation and governance committees to have formal charters addressing specific responsibilities. Nasdaq rules require all audit and most compensation committees to have formal written charters, but the nominations process can be described in either a charter or board resolutions.

That being said, charters or detailed resolutions delineating the authority of all board committees are a good practice.

15. Can boards delegate all of their authority to committees?

Not all of it. Under state corporation laws, some things can't be delegated to committees and must be retained at the full board level. Typical non-delegable powers & duties include:

- Filling board vacancies
- Authorizing dividends
- Adopting or amending bylaws
- Declaring dividends
- Authorizing the issuance of stock
- Approving a merger

Of course, committees can – and often do – play a role in all of these things.

Exchange rules also contain some limits on the ability of boards or committees to delegate authority. For example, the whole board must make independence determinations, and the audit committee cannot delegate its responsibilities to another committee.

One more point to keep in mind about committees – while the exchanges tend to focus on "independence," outside of the audit, comp and nominating/governance committees, many times a director's "disinterestedness" is of equal or greater importance from a corporate law perspective.

For example, directors may be called upon to authorize a transaction or address some other matter in which some directors of the company have a financial or other interest. In these situations, the key question isn't whether the directors making that decision are "independent" within the meaning of stock exchange rules, but whether they are "disinterested" with respect the particular matter under scrutiny.

D. Director Independence – Basics

16. Do the NYSE & Nasdaq require all directors to be independent?

Neither the NYSE nor Nasdaq requires all directors to be independent. The requirement is that a majority of the board consist of "independent" directors – as defined by the exchange.

It's important to keep in mind that it didn't used to be that way. Prior to Sarbanes-Oxley (a huge corporate governance law enacted in 2002), the exchanges generally required only a couple of independent directors as a prerequisite to listing. Many companies in that era had boards that were comprised primarily of management insiders.

Today, although only a majority of the board is required to be independent, most large companies have only a single executive (or former executive) on their boards, or at most two insiders. In fact, the CEO was the sole management insider on more than 60% of S&P 500 boards in 2016, according to Spencer Stuart's annual Board Index.

This trend reflects the governance preferences of some institutional investors and other governance mavens. For example, the Council of Institutional Investors (the primary association for institutional investors) recommends that at least two-thirds of the board be "independent" – as defined by CII's policy. CalPERS and TIAA-CREF (major public and private sector retirement fund investors) also want supermajority independence.

And as a practical matter, with the need for independent audit, compensation and nominating/governance committees, there's just not a lot of room on most boards for management insiders.

17. What independence standards should be evaluated in determining whether a director is independent?

You might need to look at quite a few standards to determine whether a director is "independent." First, there are the exchange listing standards. These include both bright line tests and more subjective, open-ended criteria.

Under the NYSE standards, boards have to determine that the director has no "material relationship" with the company - either directly or as a partner, shareholder or officer of an organization that has a relationship with the company.

Nasdaq's standards are similar – they require the board to affirmatively determine that directors have no relationship that "would interfere with the exercise of independent judgment in carrying out the responsibilities of a director."

Beyond that catch-all, there are bright-line tests. For example, The NYSE bright line tests say that you can't be independent if you've been an employee of the company within the past 3 years or an immediate family member's been an executive officer within that period.

You're also dinged if you've received more than $120k in compensation within any 12-month period during the past 3 years.

If you're currently an audit partner or employee of your outside auditor or internal auditor, you're also bounced and probably in big trouble from an independence standpoint. You're also bounced if you've got an immediate family member who is a partner at that firm.

If you were a partner or employee of your auditor within the last three years and personally worked on the listed company's audit within that time, you're also not independent (same is true if your immediate family member did this).

If you were, within the last three years, employed as an executive officer of another company where any of your company's present executive officers at the same time serves or served on that company's compensation committee, you aren't independent.

If you're a current employee, or an immediate family member is a current executive officer, of a company that has done business with the company which, in any of the last three fiscal years, exceeds the greater of $1 million, or 2% of such other company's consolidated gross revenues, then you're also out.

Nasdaq's got similar standards. There are some differences, but there not worth going into right now. The outcome of having the bright line standards together with the subjective standard is to basically say, "look, you've got to make up your own mind about independence, but if your director fits into any of these boxes, then that person can't be independent."

In addition to exchange rules, some companies adopt additional independence criteria in their corporate governance guidelines. If you have these, then you need to look at them as well when assessing independence. The most common addition in these supplemental standards is a provision disqualifying somebody as being independent if the company has made charitable contributions to an organization with which they're affiliated in excess of a specified amount.

Then there are the proxy advisory firms: ISS and Glass Lewis. They've got their own views on independence – in some ways more restrictive than the exchanges – and we'll get to them later.

If you want your compensation awards to qualify under Internal Revenue Code Section 162(m), then you need to satisfy the IRS's independence requirements. Also, if you want transactions between the company and its directors and officers to be exempt from Section 16 under Rule 16b-3, then those need to be approved by a committee of "non-employee directors" – as defined in that rule.

18. <u>What committees must be comprised of independent directors?</u>

If your company is listed on the NYSE, the audit, compensation and governance/nominating committees need to consist solely of independent directors.

Nasdaq's rules are similar, except there's some leeway for the governance/nominating committee. You can either handle nominations using a committee consisting solely of independent directors or using independent directors who constitute a majority of the board's independent directors, in a vote in which only independent directors participate.

If you're going to use the latter option, you need to have a procedure in place so that the non-independent directors know to recuse themselves from voting on director nominees. It's often easier to just use the independent committee structure.

19. What are the enhanced independence standards for audit committees?

To understand the enhanced independence standards for audit committees, you first need to look at the SEC rule that governs this topic. Rule 10A-3 of the Exchange Act, which is incorporated by reference into the NYSE and Nasdaq requirements, basically says that an audit committee member can't be an affiliate of the company (or any subsidiary), or accept directly or indirectly any consulting, advisory, or other compensatory fee from the company or its subsidiaries, other than directors' fees. That's in addition to passing all of the bright line and subjective independence tests applicable to all directors.

The SEC requires that each national securities exchange prohibit the initial or continued listing of companies that aren't in compliance with Rule 10A-3.

20. What are the enhanced independence standards for compensation committees?

Exchange Act Rule 10C-1 imposes enhanced independence criteria on compensation committee members of listed companies.

Under Rule 10C-1, the NYSE and Nasdaq adopted rules that require the board to consider all factors specifically relevant to determining whether a director has a relationship to the listed company which is material to that director's ability to be independent from management, including the source of compensation of such director – such as any consulting, advisory or other compensatory fee paid by the listed company to such director; and whether such director is affiliated with the listed company, any of its subsidiaries or subsidiary affiliates.

Just like Rule 10A-3 for audit committees, Rule 10C-1's requirements are in addition to all of the bright-line and subjective independence tests applicable to all directors.

E. Director Independence - Exchange Standards

21. What is the effect of the NYSE & Nasdaq's "bright line" independence tests?

If you can't pass the bright line tests, then no matter what kind of mental contortions the board is willing to go through, it can't decide that you're independent. But passing them doesn't let the board off the hook – it has to affirmatively determine independence based on its evaluation of relevant factors.

22. What are the primary differences between the NYSE & Nasdaq independence tests?

Maybe the most important difference is that Nasdaq provides a 180-day cure period if a listed company fails to comply with the requirement that a majority of the board be comprised of independent directors, while the NYSE does not.

I probably should clarify that if you trip-up and blow a listing requirement, the absence of a cure period doesn't mean that you're going to get kicked off the exchange that afternoon. What it does mean is that there's a delisting process that's going to be initiated, and you're going to have to address your compliance issue pronto – or else you will get delisted.

If the resignation of an independent director causes a NYSE listed company to no longer have a majority of independent directors, the company must notify the NYSE of its failure to meet a continued listing standard and file a Form 8-K under Item 3.01. A Nasdaq company has time to fix it.

Nasdaq rules also permit one non-independent director who is not an officer or employee or a family member of an officer or employee to serve on the audit, nominating or compensation committee for up to 2 years if the board of directors, under "exceptional and limited circumstances," determines that membership on the committee by that person is in the best interests of the company and its shareholders.

There are also differences in the amount of business between the company and a business with which the director is affiliated that will disqualify the director from being considered independent. The NYSE says the disqualifying amount the greater of 2% of such other company's consolidated gross revenues or $1 million during any year in the past three years. The Nasdaq says that the disqualifying amount is the greater of 5% or $200K over that same period.

23. How are various payments treated under the exchanges independence tests?

There are differences in the ways that payments are treated that can affect the independence determination. For example, in determining whether the $1 million/2%

consolidated gross revenue threshold has been exceeded, the NYSE listing standards look at the revenues of the director's company, while Nasdaq looks at the revenues of the recipient – the company that received the payments – which could be either the listed company or the director's company, depending on the transaction.

So, if the director is affiliated with a small company that is purchasing product from the much larger Nasdaq company whose board they serve on, then that person might be deemed to flunk a bright line test that wouldn't be flunked if they served on a NYSE company.

24. Are payments, loans and charitable contributions all looked at in the same way?

No, they aren't. We've already discussed the different ways that Nasdaq and the NYSE look at payments by or to companies in determining whether the bright line test has been flunked, but there are also differences in the way that charitable contributions and bank loans are treated. Charitable contributions and bank loans aren't deemed to be payments under the NYSE rules, but that's not the case under Nasdaq rules.

25. Who is required to make the independence determination under exchange rules?

The buck stops with the board of directors. The board must affirmatively determine that a majority of the board is independent. It is sort of odd that the board makes a determination about its own members, but that is the way it is.

This is something that shouldn't be a once-a-year event either. Boards need to have procedures for re-assessing director independence in the event of significant developments with respect to a director during the year that might trigger independence concerns.

In practice, most governance committees require directors to provide them with notice of any potential change in their status that might implicate the independence assessment.

F. Director Independence – Proxy Advisors

26. Do ISS and Glass Lewis simply apply the NYSE & Nasdaq independence standards?

Wouldn't that be nice! Unfortunately, the proxy advisors have their own standards. To more fully understand who the proxy advisors are and what they do, check out the "Proxy Advisors Handbook" on TheCorporateCounsel.net.

27. On what do the proxy advisory firms base their independence assessment?

Primarily, their analysis is based on what's in the proxy statement. The SEC's and NYSE/Nasdaq rules don't require proxy disclosure about every relationship that a board considered in determining that a director is independent.

In addition, the related-party transaction disclosure requirements in Item 404(a) of Regulation S-K contain both dollar ($120,000) and materiality thresholds. So, relationships that aren't disclosed in the proxy statement typically won't factor into the analyses performed by ISS and Glass Lewis.

However, to the extent you considered any of those "below the radar" relationships in making your independence assessment, those are going to have to be disclosed in the proxy statement.

28. Are their independence standards more demanding than those of the Exchanges?

They don’t take the NYSE and Nasdaq standards as gospel. They start there - and then impose their own, more demanding criteria.

In particular, ISS has a category of directors called “non-independent non-executive directors whom it doesn’t believe to be independent. Until recently, these people were referred to as “affiliated outside directors,” in the ISS policies, and you may still see people refer to them by that name. This classification can cause some complications for companies that you need to keep in mind.

Let me try to explain - in order for ISS to regard somebody as an independent director, that person must have no material connection to the company other than a board seat.

“Material” means a relationship - financial, personal or otherwise - that a reasonable person might conclude could potentially influence the director's objectivity in a manner that would have a meaningful impact on their ability to satisfy their fiduciary duties. ISS considers relationships that have existed within the five years prior to evaluation to be relevant for purposes of evaluating independence.

People with such relationships won't be classified as independent, even if they meet NYSE or Nasdaq independence criteria – instead, ISS classifies them as "non-independent non-executive directors." As a practical matter, ISS's standards come down hard on two categories of people: former CEOs of the company – who can NEVER be independent even if they're beyond the 3-year NYSE look-back, and professional service providers (lawyers, bankers, consultants) who get dinged as being affiliated if they get paid more than $10k.

What's the consequence? If any non-independent non-executive director serves on your audit, comp or governance committee, then ISS will recommend a withhold vote on that person and all of your insider directors.

Glass Lewis isn't as specific as ISS, but it also categorizes directors as "independent," "affiliated" or "inside" directors. Independent directors have no material financial, familial or other current relationships with the company, its executives or other directors except for board service and standard director fees.

It considers relationships that existed within three to five years before the inquiry to be "current" for purposes of evaluating a director's independence. Directors who own or control 20% or more of the company's stock are considered affiliates.

To be fair, not all standards imposed by proxy advisors are more demanding than the exchanges. For example, many of the tests in ISS's policy – for example, the professional services and transactional tests – look only at current relationships and do not have a lookback, unlike the NYSE and Nasdaq tests. So, when a prohibited relationship is terminated, a director can be classified as independent without having to wait three years.

29. What are the consequences of an ISS determination that a director is not "independent" under its standards?

It can result in an "against" or "withhold" vote for that director and, depending on the circumstances, others as well. The big problem is the "non-independent, non-executive director" category. If that person serves on the audit, comp or nominating/governance committees, the proxy advisors will recommend an against/withhold vote and may also recommend an against/withhold vote on other insider directors.

30. Do the proxy advisors require a "supermajority" of the board to be independent?

ISS does not, but Glass Lewis does. Glass Lewis requires boards to be two-thirds independent. Where a board is less than two-thirds independent, Glass Lewis typically recommends voting against some of the inside and/or affiliated directors in order to satisfy the two-thirds threshold.

G. D&O Questionnaires

31. What are "D&O Questionnaires"?

D&O questionnaires are questionnaires that are designed to solicit information from directors and officers of companies that is necessary to comply with the company's disclosure obligations in its 10-K & proxy statement. They are also used as part of the process of determining whether a director satisfies independence standards.

The questionnaires solicit biographical and business information, information about other directorships, information about share ownership, transactions with the company, compensation, legal & regulatory proceedings in which the director or officer was involved, and various other matters. They tend to be extremely detailed and complex, and take quite a bit of time to complete. They are also often confusing, which leads to a lot of unanswered questions

Companies also use D&O questionnaires in connection with public offerings of their securities, and as a result, those questionnaires frequently contain information about affiliations with FINRA member firms and other information that needs to be provided to FINRA in connection with its review of the underwriting arrangements for the offering under its Corporate Financing Rule.

In terms of who gets them, all directors will receive them, and most companies give them to each of their executive officers. Some go beyond this and send them to all Section 16 officers (i.e., all the officers who have to file Forms 3, 4 and 5 to report their transactions in the company's stock). This is potentially a slightly larger group due to definitional differences between Rule 3b-7 - which defines "executive officers" - and Rule 16a-1(f), which lays out the officers subject to Section 16 reporting obligations.

Some disclosure requirements also apply to departing directors and executive officers, so you need to make arrangements to have these individuals complete them, which can sometimes require some pretty advanced diplomatic skills.

32. **Who handles the process of preparing & distributing them?**

The in-house legal staff typically prepares and distributes D&O questionnaires, although they may be prepared or reviewed by outside counsel as well, depending on the company. It's important to keep these current – disclosure requirements change from year to year, so the D&O questionnaires need to be updated annually.

This is a pretty important job, but in keeping with a profession whose professional journals are edited by students, it usually devolves to the low person on the totem pole.

33. What is the process - and when are they prepared & distributed?

D&O questionnaires are typically prepared around the end of the fiscal year and are distributed to directors and officers at that time. It's one of the earliest steps in the preparation of the annual report and proxy statement.

In terms of the process, you need to review and update the document to reflect any changes in SEC or exchange rules. Because it is a complicated document, it's usually a good idea to accompany the current year's questionnaire with a copy of the individual's completed questionnaire from the prior year.

A lot of time may have gone into generating the answers to the prior year's questionnaire, and it's nice for the director or officer to be able to reply "same" to a particular question if there've been no changes.

You want to give a deadline – usually a couple of weeks if you're an accelerated filer, maybe one or two more if you're not. Expect to get them returned late and incomplete.

34. What are you supposed to do with the answers that you receive?

Well, first you review them to make sure they're complete – and to identify any areas of missing information for follow up. Then you review them closely for substance – you need to be sure that the information you're putting into the 10-K or proxy statement is consistent with an individual's responses.

You won't be reviewing this in a vacuum. Chances are pretty good that your legal and accounting staff knows the answer to many of the questions better than the individual directors & officers do. After all, you've got direct access to the compensation information, and you also have last year's D&O questionnaires to work from. If folks serve on other boards, you'll have access to their public filings (proxies, prospectuses, etc.) So, by the time you get them back, you'll have a draft of most of the disclosure that you need.

That's helpful, but it also creates a false sense of security. You must read the responses closely! Overlooking responsive information in a D&O questionnaire is a big career-limiting move.

35. Who should you contact with questions about a particular answer?

First, make sure that you do follow up – don't assume that an unanswered question means there's no changes from the prior year. There are all sorts of reasons directors and officers don't answer the form completely.

If you've ever tried to get a corporate bigwig to do anything particularly tedious, you know how difficult it is – these people are busy and they have a ton of decisions to make. No matter what, filling out your form is not a priority to them.

That brings me to my second point – you need to follow up directly with the officer or director, not allow your question to be channeled through a maze of assistants. Chances are, your boss has dealt with this issue before, and before you do anything, reach out to that person to find out if there's an established procedure for contacting a person.

Usually, I've found directors and officers to be courteous and willing to take the time to make sure that you have the information that you need in a follow up call. But be organized – get all your questions together and do this once. People don't appreciate endless follow-up calls from junior lawyers about stuff they already thought they'd addressed.

H. <u>Director Qualification Disclosures</u>

36. <u>What proxy disclosures are required about the director nomination process?</u>

Item 407(c) of Regulation S-K calls for disclosure about company's board and nominating committee and about how the nominating process works, including whether the board has a nominating committee (and if not, why not, and who handles director nominations), whether the nominating committee has a charter, whether the nominating committee has a policy to consider director candidates submitted by shareholders, minimum director nominee qualifications and more.

The thing about these disclosure requirements is that answering them in the negative doesn't look good – e.g., the Company doesn't have a nominating committee or a policy to consider director candidates submitted by shareholders. So, it's a disclosure requirement that usually compels companies to take some kind of action so that their response looks good.

37. <u>What disclosures about qualifications of directors are required by Item 407 of Regulation S-K?</u>

Item 407(c)(2)(v) requires a description of any specific minimum qualifications for nominees recommended by the nominating committee – things you often see are qualities like integrity, judgment, reputation, prior board or senior management experience, a record of achievement, etc.

You also have to disclose any specific qualities or skills that the nominating committee believes are necessary for one or more directors to possess, such as industry experience, financial/accounting expertise, engineering, legal & regulatory, international operations experience, marketing, etc.

For individual directors and director nominees, Item 401(e)(1) requires disclosure of the specific experience, qualifications, attributes or skills that led to the conclusion that the person should serve as a director at the time the disclosure is made, in light of the company's business and structure. The disclosure should specifically address the aspects of the director's or director nominee's experience, qualifications, attributes or skills that led to the conclusion that the individual should serve on the board.

The SEC gives you a lot of rope here – there's a lot of flexibility in how you comply with this disclosure requirement. But if you don't articulate why you've sought out a particular director at the time they are brought on board, it can be difficult to articulate in detail the specific qualities that a particular director brings to the table that were the specific reasons that they were asked to join the board.

38. Are companies required to have policies on shareholder submission of nominees?

No - but if you don't, you have to disclose that fact (and you look like the village idiot).

39. If companies make changes in their shareholder nomination policies, are they required to disclose them?

Yes. Any material changes to the procedures by which security holders may recommend nominees to the company's board of directors must be disclosed in its periodic Exchange Act reports.

40. Are companies required to have policies on board diversity?

No. What's required is a description of whether there is a policy about considering diversity. If so how, then you also have to disclose how the board or the committee considers it in identifying nominees for director, how the policy is implemented, and how the effectiveness of the policy is assessed.

Most companies don't have formal board diversity policies – and the SEC is so flexible about the definition of a “policy” in this context that proxy disclosure itself can serve as the policy. Companies that take diversity into account sometimes include this as a criterion for directors in their corporate governance guidelines.

The SEC does want some specificity in these disclosures – just tossing off a throwaway line about the board considering diversity isn’t going to cut it. The SEC wants disclosure about how that factors into the process.

I. <u>Shareholder Communications with Directors</u>

41. Are companies required to have procedures for shareholders to communicate with directors?

Not under SEC rules, but Item 407(f) of Regulation S-K requires companies to disclose in their proxy statements – or the company's website address where the required information may be accessed –whether or not they have such procedures in place. If so, companies are required to describe those procedures – and if not, they are required to explain why not.

NYSE-listed companies are required to disclose – either on the company's website or in the proxy statement – a method for interested parties (not just shareholders) to communicate directly with the presiding director or with the non-management or independent directors as a group so that such parties can make their concerns known to the non-management or independent directors.

Nasdaq does not have a comparable requirement.

42. Do most companies have policies regarding shareholder communications with directors?

As with other governance-type disclosure requirements, this one almost compels companies to have some sort of procedures for shareholders to communicate with directors. Otherwise, you look pretty bad.

43. What disclosures about those policies are required?

Item 407(f) of Regulation S-K requires you to describe the manner in which shareholders can send communications to the board and, if applicable, to specified individual directors.

If all security holder communications are not sent directly to board members, you also have to describe your process for determining which communications will be relayed to board members – unless that process has been approved by a majority of the independent directors.

44. Is a board's willingness to engage important to shareholders?

Yes. In fact, it's become a high priority issue for some institutional investors. It's funny – not too long ago, engagement between directors and investors was almost unheard of. But now with say-on-pay and the rise of activism, director engagement is becoming a bigger part of shareholder relations strategies. This isn't about the full board meeting with an institutional investor – just a single director in most cases.

I think that more proactive director engagement efforts came after the first round of say-on-pay votes, when people either failed or got low approval votes. You saw a lot of comp committee chairs jumping into the fray when that happened, and it has sort of grown from there.

Investors aren't insisting on having directors present in every interaction – in fact, a fair number of investors don't want to engage with directors. Or only in limited circumstances.

But there may be times when investors want to talk with a director. They may want to speak to the lead director, board chair or head of a key committee to determine whether the board is paying attention to a key issue. In some cases, they may be concerned that management is unresponsive to them. Sometimes it's because they think management hasn't responded to their concerns.

Sometimes they've got a beef with the board's performance that they want to address. So, some investors want companies to adopt procedures for director involvement in shareholder engagement.

It's challenging to include directors in the engagement process – independent directors are typically not as involved in the details of the company's operations as members of management are, and so a lot of preparation may be necessary to put a director in a position to have an effective investor meeting - or at least one where the investor's representatives don't leave scratching their heads.

Remember, investors will have done a lot of research into their areas of concern, and if the director doesn't demonstrate the same level of understanding, things can get off the rails pretty quickly.

For example, if an institutional investor has concerns about compensation, you can bet they'll have studied the compensation plans and the company's disclosures pretty carefully. If they meet with a comp committee chair who doesn't demonstrate an in-depth familiarity with them, the meeting isn't going to go well.

Of course, there are always Reg FD concerns to be taken into account as well and there needs to be prep work done here too. This is also why you almost never want a director to go to a meeting with an investor unaccompanied.

45. How do boards engage with shareholders in practice?

In one sense, there are two types of shareholder engagement. The traditional version of engagement – conducted through the CEO, CFO and IR head – typically takes place through investor communications like earnings releases, conference calls, analyst and investor one-on-ones, investor conferences, etc. These officers typically are dealing with portfolio managers within institutional investors.

Directors are very rarely involved as participants in investor conferences or similar events. If people attending the event get wind of the fact that a director is there, they will flock to that person and it will distract from the event. It's sort of like what happened when my sons played high school football at Archbishop Hoban in Akron - their school's arch rival is St. Vincent-St. Mary's, where LeBron James went to high school. LeBron always showed up for the game, and believe me, when he did, all 10,000 people in the stands had their eyes on him for much of the game.

In addition to this traditional type of engagement, there's a newer version that is mostly about corporate governance issues.

It's probably worth pointing out at this juncture something that you may not be aware of – the people who make the decision to buy or sell shares at an institutional investor usually aren't the people who decide how to vote the proxies. This latter group are the folks who scrutinize your governance practices, and decide how the institution will vote at your meeting.

The corporate secretary typically is the officer that takes the lead here, and this is where there might be an occasional engagement of a single director with a particular investor.

Most director engagement comes through responding to formal communications – such as letters from investors to the board addressing a particular issue, and through meetings between investors and an individual director (usually the lead director) or a small group of independent directors. In the ordinary course, management may well be present too.

This kind of engagement has most typically been reactive – in other words, directors have most often met with investors who've formally requested a meeting with them. But I also think this is changing – there's a developing expectation among institutional investors that directors will have a role to play in the company's engagement program, and some companies are offering up their lead director or other key board members when they reach out to investors to try to set up a meeting or a phone call.

Again, I don't want to leave the impression that investors want directors involved in all – or even most – engagements. But the fact that they're involved at all is a pretty significant change over the way things used to be.

J. Audit Committees - Meetings

46. Who should attend audit committee meetings?

The audit committee, CEO & CFO, other members of management depending on the matters to be addressed - the GC and Chief Compliance Officer are almost always in attendance, and the Director of Internal Audit is often there as well.

Outside counsel may be in attendance from time-to-time as well, particularly if there are investigations, regulatory issues or litigation that are being dealt with at the meeting.

Most or all of these people will be kicked out at some point during the meeting, so the committee can meet in executive session.

47. Do outside auditors typically attend audit committee meetings?

Yes, outside auditors are customarily present at the audit committee's meetings. When you think about it, they're kind of essential participants most of the time – a big part of the audit committee's role is to ensure the integrity of the company's financial statements. And the outside auditors play a very big role in that endeavor.

Outside auditors usually are present at the meetings, and it's important for them to be there for the committee's discussion of SEC filings, draft earnings releases, the impact of new accounting standards or proposed changes in accounting principles, internal control matters, financing and liquidity discussions, and internal audit plan status.

The outside auditors will frequently prepare their own presentations to the audit committee, which are circulated to the committee and management in advance of the meeting for discussion at the meeting. There are a bunch of required audit committee-auditor communications that get taken care of during or in advance of audit committee meetings.

48. Are there audit committee meetings that outside auditors aren't typically invited to attend?

Yes. The audit committee has a very large role. I like to think of the audit committee as sort of the "special forces" of the board of directors – if there's a tough, dirty job to do, it usually falls to the audit committee to do it.

That means they deal with a lot of stuff beyond the financial statements, including a wide variety of risk-related issues and legal & compliance matters. Often, privilege is a concern - and the presence of the independent auditors will blow a privilege claim.

49. Is the audit committee required to meet separately with the outside auditors?

NYSE companies have to periodically meet separately with the outside auditor – and they have to meet separately with management and with internal audit as well.

So, audit committee meetings have lots of executive sessions – it's common to see large groups of people parading in and out of audit committee meetings. Even though Nasdaq doesn't require this, it's a pretty common practice for those companies as well.

50. Does having outside auditors present at a meeting raise privilege concerns?

Yes, as I alluded to earlier, it does. The law here is complex. And the facts & circumstances matter a lot.

For example, if accounting principles are an issue in an investigation or in litigation, a discussion of those principles with the audit committee and its counsel might be protected - courts recognize that, in order to advise clients, lawyers need assistance in interpreting concepts that may be foreign to them, such as complex financial terms or accounting concepts.

But if you're simply getting a legal update from counsel on litigation or an investigation and your outside auditor does not have a role to play, then your privilege is in peril.

Several states recognize an accountant-client privilege. This includes, for example, Florida, Pennsylvania, Colorado and Missouri. But many other states don't - and even if you're in one that does, bear in mind that the Feds don't recognize it – so you're out of luck if you're dealing with the DOJ or SEC or in a federal court case dealing with federal claims.

K. Audit Committees - Disclosure Obligations

51. What is the relationship between the statute, SEC rules & Exchange listing requirements for audit committees?

Section 10A(m)(1) of the Exchange Act (created by Section 301 of Sarbanes-Oxley) requires the SEC to direct, by rule, that the national securities exchanges prohibit the listing of any security of an company that is not in compliance with several enumerated standards regarding audit committees.

Rule 10A-3 under the Exchange Act implements Section 301's requirements. It requires audit committees to be comprised of independent directors, mandates that they be directly responsible for the appointment, compensation, retention and oversight of the work of the outside auditors, requires them to establish procedures for confidential complaints about accounting, internal controls or auditing matters, must have the authority to retain counsel, and must be appropriately funded by the company.

Rule 10A-3's requirements apply only to listed companies, and they are embedded in the NYSE and Nasdaq's listing requirements.

52. **Are audit committees required to have a "financial expert"? What disclosures are required concerning audit committee financial experts?**

Audit committees aren't required to have someone who is a "financial expert." Item 407 of Reg S-K requires disclosure of whether there is an "audit committee financial expert" on the committee - and, if not, why not.

The exchanges require each member of the audit committee to be financially literate, and at least one member of the audit committee must have accounting or related financial management expertise, but those qualification requirements are different than the ones the SEC requires in order for someone to be regarded as an "audit committee financial expert" under Item 407.

53. **Are audit committees required to be independent? What disclosures about independence are required?**

Audit committees are NOT required to be independent – only those of companies listed on national securities exchanges are subject to the requirements of Rule 10A-3 and the exchanges' listing standards on independence.

I don't want to leave you with the wrong impression. Unless you work with a bunch of small caps that aren't listed, almost every company you encounter is going to have an independent audit committee – because most of them are listed somewhere.

Item 407 requires companies to identify in their proxy statements each director and nominee for director, who is independent under the independence standards applicable to the company. You also have to disclose the standards you use in making an independence assessment.

For each director and nominee for director that a company identifies as independent, it must describe, by specific category or type, any transactions, relationships or arrangements not disclosed pursuant to Item 404(a) that were considered by the board of directors under the applicable independence definitions in determining that the director is independent.

Now, there are some exceptions from the independence requirement for audit committees– there are transitional provisions that apply to IPO companies that give them a little time to get into full compliance with the audit committee independence requirement, and there's an "exceptional and limited circumstances" exemption that comes into play sometimes for Nasdaq companies.

If you avail yourself of an exemption, you have to identify the nature of the relationship that makes a particular individual non-independent and the reasons for the board's determination.

54. Are audit committees required to have charters? What disclosures about the charter are required?

SEC rules don't require a charter – but NYSE and Nasdaq listing standards do. So, most audit committees have them.

Item 407 of Reg S-K requires disclosure of whether the audit committee has a charter. If there is a charter, Instruction 2 to Item 407 requires it be posted on the corporate website or included as an appendix to the proxy statement every 3 years (or if it's been materially amended).

If it is on the website, companies need to disclose that and provide the company's Web site address. If you don't post the charter on your website, and you aren't required to include it as an appendix, then you've got to identify in which of the prior fiscal years the charter was so included in satisfaction of this requirement.

This is a pain in the neck. Post the darn thing on your website.

55. What disclosure about audit committee oversight of the auditor is required?

Actually, none. The proxy rules require you to include disclosure of information under Item 407 about whether the audit committee has discussed with the auditor its independence & other matters - but disclosure about the committee's oversight responsibilities isn't required. Nevertheless, you see a lot of voluntary disclosure about this kind of thing, because investors care about it.

L. Audit Committees - Financial Experts

56. What is an "audit committee financial expert"? Do SEC rules require companies to have one or more of them?

An "audit committee financial expert" is defined in Item 407 of S-K, and the definition is pretty elaborate.

Everybody take a deep breath - An audit committee financial expert means someone who has an understanding of GAAP and financial statements; the ability to assess the general application of those principles in connection with the accounting for estimates, accruals and reserves; experience preparing, auditing, analyzing or evaluating financial statements that present a breadth and level of complexity of accounting issues that are generally comparable to the issues that can reasonably be expected to be raised by the company's financial statements, or experience actively supervising one or more persons engaged in such activities; an understanding of internal control over financial reporting; and an understanding of audit committee functions.

That's a mouthful – and if you don't have one, you have to disclose why you don't. Some companies have audit committees that are only comprised of financial experts!

57. **Does an audit committee financial expert need to be independent?**

If your company is listed on an exchange, the answer is yes. If it's not, then the answer's no – but you need to disclose whether that person is independent or not.

58. **In order to qualify as a financial expert, does a person need to have audit experience?**

That's not the only way you can qualify, but it certainly is the most direct path.

The SEC also requires the financial expert to have acquired those attributes through education and experience as a principal financial officer, principal accounting officer, controller, public accountant or auditor or experience in performing similar functions; actively supervising somebody in one of these positions; experience overseeing or assessing the performance of companies or public accountants with respect to the preparation, auditing or evaluation of financial statements; or – and here's the fun one – "other relevant experience."

What's "other relevant experience?" I have seen situations where companies have relied on the "other relevant experience" prong to conclude that the experience gained from being a financial analyst, an accounting or finance academic, & service as a senior financial regulator qualify a person as an "audit committee financial expert."

59. **Do audit committee members that meet Exchange requirements for financial sophistication or expertise qualify as financial experts under SEC rules?**

Not necessarily. Those requirements are not as elaborate or as detailed as the SEC's financial expert definition. I've sometimes wondered if you could have a situation that's sort of the reverse of this – where somebody might qualify as an "audit committee financial expert" but not meet the NYSE's requirement that at least one director must have accounting or related financial management expertise.

60. **Does a company with more than one audit committee financial expert have to disclose the names of each one?**

No, you can have more than one - but Item 407 requires you to only name one. If you name more, then you have to also disclose whether those folks are independent.

M. Audit Committees - Financial Literacy

61. What does it mean to be "financially literate"? What's the source of the requirement that audit committee members be financially literate?

That's a good question. In fact, there's not really any objective definition of the term that everybody can agree on. Nasdaq defines "financially literate" as being able to read and understand fundamental financial statements, including a company's balance sheet, income statement and cash flow statement. But nobody really knows what that means, and there's no comparable NYSE definition of the term.

The financial literacy requirement came from recommendations by a "blue ribbon" panel, drawing members from the business, financial and accounting communities, was established in September 1998 by the NYSE & Nasdaq to make recommendations on strengthening the role of audit committees in overseeing the corporate financial reporting process.

It was created in response to concerns expressed by SEC Chair Arthur Levitt about the adequacy of the oversight of the audit process by independent corporate directors.

Interestingly, the NYSE rules give audit committee members time to get up to speed and become financially literate if they aren't when they join the committee. The requirement is that they become financially literate within a "reasonable time." The Nasdaq doesn't – Nasdaq Rule 5605(c)(2)(A) requires companies to certify that have at least three members, each of whom is able to read and understand fundamental financial statements. There is no grace period.

62. <u>Who is required to make that determination?</u>

Commentary in the NYSE's "Listed Company Manual" suggests that the full board has to ultimately decide whether a member of the committee is financially literate, but in practice, it's usually the individual director who determines whether they are financially literate.

Best practice here is to provide some sort of self-assessment tool to committee members or prospective committee members. There are a number of these tools available.

There's no specific requirement for the board to adopt formal resolutions about financial literacy, but clearly there should be some written memorialization of the board's decision in the minutes.

Note that there isn't an annual requirement to reconfirm a director's financial literacy – although companies may wish to consider some reconfirmation procedures applicable to directors who continue to serve beyond typical retirement ages.

63. **Does the literacy requirement need to be laid out in the charter?**

Nasdaq companies have to – their charters are required to lay out membership requirements, and this is one of them.

Included in the committee composition requirements in Rule 5605(c)(2)(A) is the requirement that each member be able to read and understand fundamental financial statements.

64. **What kind of disclosure do companies have to make about financial literacy?**

Nothing in the proxy statements, but NYSE companies have to address the financial literacy of audit committee members in the annual written affirmations that they provide after the annual meeting.

65. **If an audit committee member is financially literate, does that mean the director is also a financial expert?**

No – and technically, vice versa. However, it's almost inconceivable that somebody could qualify as an audit committee financial expert and not qualify as financially literate. Only senior law firm partners, such as myself, rise to that level of utter vacuousness.

N. Auditor Engagement

66. What role does the audit committee play in the engagement - and oversight - of outside auditors?

Under Rule 10A-3, the audit committee must engage the auditors directly and is directly responsible for oversight of their work.

This includes responsibility for resolving disagreements between management and the auditor regarding financial reporting) for the purpose of preparing or issuing an audit report or performing other audit, review or attest services for the listed company, and each such registered public accounting firm must report directly to the audit committee.

67. Can management hire the auditors and simply ask the audit committee to ratify the appointment?

No. The audit committee has to be the one doing the hiring. Ministerial stuff associated with the retention can be done by officers. For instance, once the audit committee has retained an auditor and established the terms of its engagement, the CEO or another executive could sign the engagement letter.

68. Are there SEC rules governing what's required in an audit firm engagement letter?

The SEC doesn't have rules governing this, but the PCAOB does. So what's the PCAOB? It's the Public Accounting Oversight Board, a private, non-profit entity established by Sarbanes-Oxley that's responsible for providing regulatory oversight to audits of public companies. The PCAOB is technically a private-sector entity, but it's overseen by the SEC, which among other things appoints its members and sets its budget.

Anyway, Appendix C to the PCAOB's Auditing Standard #16 requires auditors to address matters relating to the purpose of the audit, the auditor's responsibilities, and management's responsibilities. While the SEC doesn't specify what's required in an engagement letter, it does prohibit indemnification in connection with audits.

69. Are companies required to obtain shareholder approval for the audit committee's decision to hire an auditor?

No - and a requirement to obtain shareholder approval would likely run afoul of Rule 10A-3's requirement that the audit committee be solely responsible for retaining an auditor.

Still, most companies do conduct a shareholder vote – and the reason for this is to ensure that they have a quorum for the meeting, because this is one of the few remaining matters that brokers can vote on.

Beginning in 2010, exchange rules were revised to allow brokers to vote shares without their customers' direction only for "routine" matters when the proposal is supported by management, but were prohibited from voting for "non-routine" matters.

The election of directors was specifically defined as non-routine. The NYSE rules, particularly, were tightened further in January 2012, when the following matters were designated as non-routine: proposals to de-stagger the board of directors, majority voting in the election of directors, eliminating supermajority voting requirements, providing for the use of consents, providing rights to call a special meeting and certain types of anti-takeover provision overrides.

Auditor ratification, however, continues to be regarded as a routine matter for which brokers may vote uninstructed shares.

Because both exchanges preclude brokers from voting uninstructed shares for matters that aren't routine, their votes usually don't count towards a quorum under state law at meetings limited to routine matters. That's because quorum requirements often require the presence of a specified number of shares that are "entitled to vote" at the meeting.

So, if you don't have a routine matter on the ballot, you risk not receiving a quorum your annual meeting. Auditor ratification is pretty innocuous as proposals go, and fits the bill nicely for quorum purposes.

70. If shareholders vote against ratification, must the audit committee choose a different auditor?

No, this is a non-binding vote. Otherwise, it would run afoul of the requirement that the audit committee remain in charge of hiring and firing the auditor. Most companies indicate that they will consider the results of the vote in deciding whether to retain the auditor.

O. Audit Committees - Pre-Approval

71. What are the requirements applicable to audit committee pre-approval of non-audit services by the independent auditor?

Section 202 of Sarbanes-Oxley, as implemented by SEC rules (Rule 2-01 of Regulation S-X), requires audit committees to pre-approve all audit, review and attest services, and all other permissible non-audit services to be rendered by the company's independent auditor.

72. What methods of pre-approval are permitted?

Before the auditor is engaged to provide a non-audit service, the engagement must be either approved by the audit committee on a service by service basis (either at the time the committee approves the annual audit or when the need arises) or authorized under the terms of pre-approval policies and procedures established by the committee that are detailed as to the particular service, require the audit committee to be informed of each service, and don't delegate audit committee responsibilities to management.

The audit committee may also delegate authority to one or more committee members to grant pre-approvals for particular services. These preapprovals have to be reported to the full committee at its meetings.

73. **Do most companies adopt formal pre-approval policies?**

Yes, most companies opt for this approach. These policies typically lay out pre-approval requirements and procedures for specific services on an engagement-by-engagement basis for unanticipated service needs arising during the year.

They may also address things like deviations from agreed upon fees, limitations on delegated authority, procedures that must be followed by management before a request for preapproval of a non-audit service may be made, management reporting requirements with respect to authorized services, and other matters.

Item 9(e)(5) of Schedule 14A requires disclosure of the audit committee's pre-approval policies and procedures. Companies can either include a copy of their policy and procedures - or provide “clear, concise and understandable descriptions” (per SEC Adopting Release No. 33-8183 from 2003). Most companies opt to provide a description.

74. Can authority to pre-approve non-audit services be delegated?

Yes - and it frequently is. The audit committee chair (or some subset of audit committee members) may be delegated the authority to approve non-audit services.

There are often limitations on this delegated authority – for example, it may be limited to services not exceeding a specific dollar amount. Delegating authority to a member of management, however, is a big "no-no."

75. Are there limitations on the types of non-audit services that an auditor can provide?

Yes, there are certain tax services that are prohibited by the PCAOB's rules and there are some limitations and specific disclosure requirements to the committee that apply to proposed engagements for certain other tax services.

In addition, there are services that the SEC says will impair auditor independence and are prohibited. These include:

- Bookkeeping
- Financial information systems design and implementation
- Appraisal or valuation services, fairness opinions, or contribution-in-kind reports

- Actuarial services
- Internal audit outsourcing services
- Management functions or human resources
- Broker-dealer, investment adviser, or investment banking services
- Legal services and expert services unrelated to the audit

In addition to the specific prohibited services, audit committees should consider whether any service provided by the audit firm may impair the firm's independence in fact or appearance.

P. Change in Auditors

76. How often do companies typically change their outside auditors?

Not often. It is a big and fairly disruptive event - and often prompts investor concerns about the reasons for the change. Unfortunately, when auditors are changed, the reasons are sometimes ominous, and investors know that and often think the worst.

77. What reporting requirements are there when a change is made?

There are a myriad of disclosure and other requirements following the dismissal or resignation of a company's current auditor. Disclosure relating to changes in—and disagreements with—independent accountants is elicited by Item 304 of Regulation S-K.

Briefly, Item 304(a) asks for disclosures about the auditor change, including whether there were any disagreements, while Item 304(b) calls for more disclosure about any such disagreements with the former auditor.

You have to provide a lot of detail about the circumstances of the termination - whether auditor resigned, declined to stand for re-election or was dismissed, and the date it was terminated.

You also have to disclose if the auditor's PCAOB certification was revoked. Any adverse opinion, or disclaimer or modification of opinion in the auditor's opinion in the past 2 years also needs to be disclosed. You have to disclose whether decision to change auditors was recommended by audit committee (or full board, if board has no such committee),

You also need to disclose whether there were any reportable events. Specifically, this means that you need to disclose whether:

1. Auditor has concluded that material weakness in internal controls exists.
2. Auditor is no longer willing to rely on management's representations, or was otherwise unwilling to associate itself with company's financial statements.
3. Auditor has advised company that audit scope needs to be significantly expanded or other information has arisen that, if further investigated, might materially impact previous audit reports or their underlying financial statements.
4. Auditor has advised company that information has arisen that materially impacts previous audit reports or their underlying financial statements.

This disclosure is called for in four Exchange Act filings:

- Item 4.01 of Form 8-K (Item 304(a))
- Item 9 of Part II of Form 10-K (Item 3034(b))
- Rule 14a-3(b)(4) for the glossy annual report (Item 304(b))
- Item 9(d) of Schedule 14A for the proxy statement (Item 304(a))

Item 304 disclosure also is required by Forms S-1 and S-4, and by Item 14 of Form 10.

Things get very messy if the company and its auditor have had "disagreements" about internal controls or financial reporting. Regulation S-K Item 304(a)(iv) defines a disagreement as one occurring "at the decision-making level (i.e., between personnel of the company responsible for presentation of its financial statements and personnel of the accounting firm responsible for rendering its report").

That S-K Item's Instructions state that disagreements are "interpreted broadly" and "includes any difference of opinion concerning any matter of accounting principles or practices, financial statement disclosure, or auditing scope or procedure which" (if not resolved) would need to be disclosed in the auditor's report.

If there are disagreements with the auditor, then there's a lot more to say in the 8-K. You need to identify the issue, and describe views of new auditor on each such issue. You also need to state whether former auditor was consulted on any such issue, and if so, summarize former auditor's view.

In addition, Nasdaq and NYSE standards require companies to make prompt public disclosure of a decision to change auditors, and termination of auditors and retention of new auditors can trigger multiple 8-K requirements

78. Who makes the decision to change auditors?

If a company decides to change auditors, that decision has to be made by its audit committee under Rule 10A-3. But sometimes, it's the auditors who decide to pull the plug.

Typically, at least where termination is initiated by the company, the company informs the outgoing accountant of its decision well in advance of the effective date of termination. But the Form 8-K is not due until four business days after the effective date of the termination (i.e., dismissal) of the former accountant.

Most of the Big 4 auditors have an internal policy that requires their clients to file a Form 8-K (complying with Item 304(a)) as soon as the firm is informed of its dismissal.

Companies typically do what the accountants want here. They need to remain on good terms with the outgoing accountant during the transition period, and get its cooperation in providing both the "termination letter" that the company must file with its Form 8-K, and the consents that will need to be included in its next two 10-Ks in order to use the accountant's audits in any 1933 Act registration statements.

If an early Form 8-K is filed, the Corp Fin Staff (the part of the SEC that reviews disclosure documents) usually will issue a comment letter requiring the company to file a Form 8-K/A within four business days after the effective date, confirming the accountant's dismissal.

The resignation or dismissal of an independent accountant, or its refusal to stand for re-appointment, is a reportable event separate from the engagement of a new independent accountant. On some occasions, two reports on Form 8-K are required for a single change in accountants, the first on the resignation (or refusal to stand for re-appointment) or dismissal of the former accountant, and the second when the new accountant is engaged

79. <u>How do investors typically react to a decision to change auditors?</u>

This is the kind of news that prompts a lot of concern from investors, and it often creates a real investor relations challenge. If the reasons for the change are bad, it's potentially catastrophic – and even if they're not, investors get nervous. It's funny, because now some good governance types have recommended rotating audit firms. Their contention is that the relationship between long-term auditors and companies is too cozy.

80. Are auditors required to make any filings in connection with a decision to terminate them - or a decision by them to resign?

Yes. They need to file a termination letter under Item 304 of S-K stating whether they agree with the company's disclosures in its 8-K filing.

That letter is due within 10 days – and the company has to amend the 8-K to include it within 2 business days of receipt. If the auditor declines to provide it, the company must disclose that fact in the 8-K.

Q. Audit Committees - Whistleblower Procedures

81. What requires audit committees to implement whistleblower procedures?

Section 301 of Sarbanes-Oxley – and Exchange Act Rule 10A-3(b)(3) – require audit committees to establish procedures for: receipt, retention and treatment of complaints received by the company regarding accounting, internal accounting controls or auditing matters; and confidential, anonymous submission by employees of concerns about questionable accounting or auditing matters.

These are commonly referred to as "whistleblower procedures," although whistleblower procedures commonly cover all types of complaints/concerns - not just those that are accounting-related.

Like the independence rules, this stuff gets incorporated into the listing requirements of the exchanges. Section 301 of Sarbanes-Oxley – and Exchange Act Rule 10A-3(b)(3) - apply to listed companies through NYSE Section 303A.06 and Nasdaq Rule 5605(c)(3).

82. What's the scope of the audit committee's responsibility? Can it delegate authority to administer the program?

The audit committee is permitted to use employees such as internal audit, in-house counsel, HR, compliance personnel and/or third parties to assist in various aspects of the process as long as it retains oversight responsibility and employee confidentiality and anonymity are preserved.

The rule doesn't require audit committees to be involved in the review and handling of complaints or their disposition. In fact, most audit committees delegate the task of receiving, classifying and responding to complaints to compliance or in-house counsel - subject to specified parameters based on the complaint's nature and potential materiality.

In other words, there's got to be a limit on delegation – criteria for kicking issues upstairs to the audit committee have to be established. Whistleblower programs usually incorporate complaint classification procedures that call for certain complaints to be reported immediately to the committee.

That's because the audit committee has sole responsibility for receiving, handling and investigating of these complaints. In implementing a whistleblower program, it's important to keep in mind that the perception that the audit committee is running the show is just as important as the reality.

This perception is likely to be compromised if potential whistleblowers believe that management will be involved in the process even though – in reality – all actions of employees and third parties will be directed and overseen by the audit committee.

Getting potential whistleblowers to focus on the "Great & Powerful Oz" and to "pay no attention to the man behind the curtain" is by far the most significant factor influencing the success or failure of the company's whistleblower program.

83. Does every complaint need to be reported to the audit committee?

No. The rule doesn't require the committee to receive the complaints directly or indirectly; it merely requires the committee to establish procedures. However, the committee has oversight responsibilities and should receive regular summaries of all accounting/auditing complaints, and discuss with appropriate steps with management to address any complaints that are legitimate.

Audit committees have complete discretion to determine the procedures for dealing with the complaints that they receive. However, it is typical (and a best practice) for the audit committee to receive regular reports with details concerning complaints (often subcategorized by number, type & source), as well as information about the status of any investigation into those complaints.

84. Must the whistleblower procedures cover matters beyond accounting matters?

No, Sarbanes-Oxley only requires procedures relating to complaints about accounting, accounting controls and audit matters.

However, companies may - and commonly do - use their SOX 301-compliant procedures for all types of complaints addressed in their codes of conduct and other policies.

85. Should whistleblower procedures be publicly disclosed? Do all whistleblower complaints have to be handled confidentially?

No. Remember, we're talking about the Great & Powerful Oz here – pay no attention to the man behind the curtain. The problem with public disclosure is that, inevitably, management is going to be involved in the implementation of the program.

Even though the audit committee will be running the show, the perception of management involvement in the reporting and investigative process will have a chilling effect on the willingness of employees to report.

In terms of confidentiality, the rule only requires employees to be able to report on an anonymous and confidential basis. Others are not required to be protected in this fashion, and with good reason – anonymity can make it very difficult to effectively investigate a claim.

R. Proxy Season - Basics

86. What is the "proxy season"?

The proxy season is the time of year when the bulk of companies are preparing their annual disclosure documents (10-Ks, annual reports & proxies) and preparing for their annual meetings of shareholders. These are the 3-4 months after a company's fiscal year end.

It is a particularly busy time not only for in-house lawyers, who typically bear the brunt of the effort to prepare these materials (especially the proxy statement), but also for many outside counsel, since they may be involved in reviewing bunches of annual disclosure documents and proxy statements for their public company clients.

87. What is the timeline of it?

Most companies have December 31st fiscal year-ends - and the timing of their proxy statements and annual meetings is driven in large part by the desire to have the proxy statements completed in time for them to be incorporated by reference into the 10-K.

Under the SEC's rules, you're allowed to incorporate required disclosures about your directors & executive officers, beneficial ownership, compensation and certain other disclosures into your 10-K by reference. But only if you get your act together and file final (known as "definitive") proxy materials within 120 days of your fiscal year end.

What this means is that a big part of Corporate America is doing their proxy statements and getting their annual meetings set up during the first four or five months of the year.

So, proxy season has generally been regarded as from January until late May or early June. That being said, parts of it are year-round.

For example, with "say-on-pay," the proxy advisors solicit input on their policies for the next proxy season during the summer months. So, just as soon as you've put down your pen, you'll be picking it up again to prepare to deal with their proposed policy changes.

Also, it used to be that you'd engage your institutional investors – at least the voting side of the house – when you were soliciting proxies. That's much more of a year-round process now, and it's real difficult to get a hearing with a lot of investors during proxy season.

What's more, with the growth in activism, you need to proactively engage with your shareholders and address their concerns. The same is true with proxy advisors – if you need to get in front of them, you'll want to do so before you're out soliciting proxies or even filing proxy material.

88. Who are all the players?

From the top down, you've got your board & execs, who'll need to complete D&O questionnaires to give you the information you'll need to get the proxy statement finalized. They'll also be given a near-final version of the document to review.

The compensation committee and its compensation advisor will be involved in preparing the CD&A. People in HR will also be involved in generating the compensation information you'll need for the tables – if you're lucky, these people know the rules and can give you your compensation tables in a form that you can drop in to the proxy statement.

You'll also have the working group within the law department who are going to likely have the responsibility for keeping the master and drafting most of the narrative disclosure.

You'll also be working with your proxy solicitor throughout the process – especially if you have items that require a supermajority vote or you've had problems with say on pay or director withhold votes. You may be interacting with ISS if there's a compensation proposal on the table in order to get some insight into how they will address it.

You'll be coordinating with your IR group on reviewing the annual report that will be included with the proxy, and spending time making sure the CEO's letter doesn't promise to achieve total global domination or some equally regrettable turn of phrase.

If you've got a contested situation, then you'll also be dealing with activists and their lawyers and advisors – and everybody else's role will be ramped up. Your investor relations people and outside corporate communications advisors will take on a particularly significant role here.

The SEC will certainly play a role in any contested situation – they really do wear a striped shirt and have a whistle in their mouths in these situations. But they can seriously throw a monkey wrench into your ordinary course annual meeting process as well – if you have to file preliminaries and they pull those for review, your whole finely tuned annual meeting schedule could be thrown into jeopardy.

89. How has the proxy season changed over the years?

It's dramatically different than it used to be. Mostly, proxy statements were a formality – until about the turn of the 21st century, the proxy advisors really weren't a factor. Institutional investors were quiescent - and annual meetings were non-events.

Going back into the '80s and early 1990s, your proxy statement might only be 10-15 pages long. I remember some that had fewer than 10 pages. You usually only used a proxy solicitor if you were dealing with a proxy contest. None of the compensation consultants were around. Can you imagine? This all reflects the seismic shift in corporate power that we've seen over the past generation away from boards - and to investors.

90. What can you do for stress relief?

When I was a young associate, we always used to like to play "Come the Revolution!" with the firm's phone directory, and decide who among the partners we'd send to the guillotine - and who would merely end up at Devil's Island. Works wonders – and it's easily transferred to a corporate law department setting.

S. Annual Meetings - Basics

91. Is a company required to hold an annual meeting?

Yes. State corporate law requires an annual shareholders meeting for the election of directors. NYSE & Nasdaq rules also require listed companies to hold annual meetings.

92. What are the rules governing the conduct of an annual meeting?

There's not a lot of guidance in the corporate law or in case law about how to conduct an annual meeting – but what authority there is suggests that the key principle is reasonableness and fairness.

Some companies have bylaw provisions that provide an outline of how business will be conducted at the annual meeting, but these tend to be more focused on the agenda and not to get into the weeds about the details of a meeting.

Even if their bylaws are silent, companies often set rules of conduct that will apply to the meeting. These often cover meeting room admission procedures, prohibition of recording or photography, the order of business to be addressed at the meeting, rules that will apply to speakers – such as limiting them to shareholders and proxies, setting forth procedures for being recognized, imposing limits on the number of individual questions and the time period that people may speak.

93. **What's the difference between an annual meeting and a special meeting?**

An annual meeting is typically a statutory requirement. Section 213 of the Delaware General Corporation Law generally requires companies to hold an annual meeting for the purpose of electing directors. Companies that are permitted to act by majority written consent can do this through a consent action, subject to some notice requirements.

If a Delaware corporation hasn't held an annual meeting for more than 13 months, a shareholder can go into the Chancery Court and ask it to order one to be held, which the court ultimately will.

While any other business can be conducted at an annual meeting, if something that requires shareholder approval arises at other times during the year, the corporation may decide to call a special meeting of shareholders.

These meetings may be called by the board or the persons authorized in the certificate or bylaws. Many companies contain provisions authorizing shareholders to call a special meeting – the thresholds typically range from holders of 10% to the holders of 50% of the outstanding shares.

94. Who has the right to attend an annual meeting?

Only shareholders of record - and their duly authorized proxies - have a legal right to attend the meeting. Some companies police attendance fairly closely, while others do not.

95. What matters must be addressed at an annual meeting?

That depends on state corporate law, but generally the one thing that has to be addressed at the annual meeting is the election of directors. Many states also require a list of shareholders be available for review at the meeting as well.

In practice, companies can address whatever they want to get shareholder approval for at an annual meeting. In order to ensure that there's at least one "routine" matter for which brokers are entitled to vote – and avoid any quorum issues – most companies ask their shareholders to ratify their auditors in addition to whatever else is on the ballot.

T. Annual Meetings - Preparation

96. Who determines the agenda?

In the ordinary course, the agenda for an annual meeting is determined by the board and management. However, shareholders can also play a part in determining the agenda through the shareholder proposal process.

Most companies have advance notice bylaws that shareholders need to comply with in order to bring a matter before the meeting.

Typical advance notice bylaw requires that shareholders submit to the corporate secretary notice of all director nominations and business to be put to a vote at an annual meeting within a 30-day window that opens and closes on specified deadlines determined by reference to the anniversary date of the prior year's annual meeting date.

This notice usually must be accompanied by fairly detailed information about the nominee or business, and the proposing shareholder.

If you comply with an advance notice bylaw, you can present your proposal or nominee at the annual meeting, but if you want to solicit proxies, you've historically had to prepare your own proxy statement.

In the past, if shareholders wanted to get their proposal into management's proxy statement, their sole recourse was Rule 14a-8. However, there are limitations on the ability of shareholders to include proposals under Rule 14a-8 – most notably, it can't be used for a proxy contest.

In recent years, shareholders have pushed for proxy access bylaws allowing them to make director nominations through the company's proxy statement if they satisfy certain conditions.

Proxy access bylaws typically enable a shareholder or a group of up to 20 shareholders who have held 3% of the company's stock for 3 years to nominate up to 20% of the board. Those nominees would be included in management's proxy statement and on its proxy card.

These bylaws have rapidly become common at larger companies. Most of the S&P 500 have some kind of access bylaw in place.

97. What preparations should be made for an annual meeting? Are they different if you've received a shareholder proposal?

There's a lot to prepare – you've got to arrange a venue well in advance, and address any security arrangements that may be necessary.

If you're inviting the media, you'll need to put together some sort of media kit. You need to determine whether you are going to establish admission procedures or otherwise limit attendance at the meeting. You need to prepare whatever audio-visual materials will be used.

You need to prepare a script for the meeting, and determine who the speakers will be at the meeting. Management remarks will need to be prepared. You need to identify and prepare responses for likely shareholder questions at the meeting. You need to figure out how you're going to deal with unexpected events.

If you receive a shareholder proposal, you need to coordinate with the shareholder the ground rules for the presentation of the proposal at the meeting. For example, when - and how - will the proponent be recognized? Who will speak for the proponent? How long will the proponent be permitted to speak about the proposal?

Sometimes, there's hostility among management toward the proponent. It is in everyone's interest to leave that at the door and work cooperatively to ensure a smooth meeting.

If a proposal is controversial or the company is otherwise in a tough spot – you really need to pay attention to security considerations at the meeting.

98. Who should be involved in preparing for the meeting?

The corporate secretary, legal department, investor relations, any member of the board or management who will have a speaking part or who may respond to questions (for directors, this typically means committee chairs), outside counsel, outside investor relations and public relations advisors, individuals responsible for marketing events, corporate security personnel – it's a big group.

99. What should a script for the meeting address? How is it prepared?

Scripts should cover the waterfront – all comments during the formal part of the meeting should be included in the script. Introductory matters addressed in scripts typically include calling the meeting to order, referring to the agenda and any rules of conduct that will apply to the meeting order, introductions of directors, management, inspectors of election, independent auditors and any other VIPs, etc.

The script's most important role is to ensure that the meeting is properly conducted in accordance with legal requirements. It will recite the presence of a quorum (usually referencing reports from the inspectors of election). The script will state the order of business to be addressed at the meeting followed by presentation of those agenda items. It will include separate announcements of the opening and closing of the polls on each matter, call for an "Inspector of Elections" report and announcement of preliminary voting results, and provide for adjournment of the meeting.

If shareholder proposals are to be made, the script should also include language recognizing the speaker. A script should also include alternative scenarios and options for addressing unanticipated proposals from the floor, possible disruptions and other events not on the agenda including emergency situations.

The script doesn't end with the end of the formal part of the meeting – it will also include management's presentation and answers to potential questions and identification of speakers.

There have been some amazing unscripted events at annual meetings over the years, but my favorite story is about Xerox's Joe Wilson at the company's 1959 annual meeting.

Xerox was the Apple/Google/Microsoft of its day, and it introduced its first copier - the Xerox 914 - at the meeting. Shareholders and the media were in attendance, and there was a machine on stage.

Back then, copiers were fed with rolls of paper, which were cut to size by the machine. Wilson's script called for him to demonstrate the copier. It was a prototype, and there were some glitches. The machine copied fine – but apparently the blade didn't work, and the blasted thing wouldn't stop copying.

Wilson found himself with his breakthrough product running amok with an auditorium full of shareholders and the press. So, what did he do? Apparently, without missing a beat, he grabbed the paper and paraded the uncut sheet down the middle aisle of the auditorium, encouraging shareholders to see for themselves the quality of the copies it made.

Meanwhile, Xerox minions scrambled to unplug the machine as inconspicuously as possible.

The 914 went on to be one of the most successful and innovative products in business history. You can even see one in the Smithsonian.

100. <u>Who should attend the meeting?</u>

All of the directors and executive officers, the corporate secretary, the GC if that person isn't the corporate secretary, outside auditors (your proxy statement will usually contain disclosure saying that they'll attend), IR staff, security. If media is going to be invited, communications personnel should also be in attendance.

U. Annual Meetings - Admission Requirements

101. Why do some companies require shareholders to register & obtain admission tickets for annual meetings?

A lot of it has to do with logistics. Some companies attract a large crowd, and they need to have a handle on how many people to expect. It's also a way to deter non-shareholders from attending – by making clear that there are admission procedures that will need to be followed, people who might want to attend for freebies or to disrupt the meeting may be discouraged.

You can also use the registration process to identify which shareholders will be attending, and perhaps whether you might expect agenda-driven questioning from some of them. Also, if you get an unexpectedly large response - that may tell you that you need to ramp up security and prepare for some bumps during the meeting.

102. What best practices should companies follow if they want to impose admission requirements?

Do it in advance! If you try & institute admission procedures without warning on the day of the meeting, you'll have chaos. Make sure you've disclosed the fact that there will be admission requirements and specify what they are in your proxy materials. You should also keep in mind the investor relations issues involved with admission procedures – if they're too cumbersome, you're going to annoy your shareholders, almost all of whom are beneficial, and not record, holders of your shares.

If you plan to issue admission tickets/cards in advance of the meeting, include instructions in the proxy materials as to how to request them. Some companies take the alternative of including admission tickets in proxy materials may include admission tickets for registered shareholders. Some treat the "Notice of Internet Availability of Proxy Materials" (also known as "notice & access") as a ticket.

If you provide for advance registration but don't plan to issue admission tickets before the meeting, require the shareholder/proxy holder to submit their request to attend and their credentials so that you can pre-clear them, and then develop a master list of RSVPs (including guests).

103. Are there specific proxy disclosure requirements that you have to follow?

No, there's nothing in the SEC's proxy rules that addresses admission requirements. But as I've said, if you're going to implement them, you want to clearly address those procedures in your proxy statement. And you need to balance your need to know who is coming and how many people will be there with the need not to make it too difficult for your shareholders to attend their meeting.

104. Do you have to enforce your admission procedures?

No, you don’t. You can always decide to relax your admission requirements after they've been disclosed in your proxy materials – and companies often do. But for purposes of advance communications and proxy disclosures, you should assume that the requirements will be strictly enforced to facilitate your ability to control the meeting.

105. Can you exclude a shareholder who doesn’t comply from the meeting?

No. Shareholders - and their duly appointed proxies - have the legal right to attend the meeting. However, they are the only ones who have that right, and you may exclude anyone else that you want.

In administering your admission procedures, you need to make sure that no shareholder is turned away inadvertently. Issues concerning shareholder status should be handled courteously & diplomatically, with a strong bias toward allowing a person who claims to be a shareholder to attend the meeting, even if they lack the proper credentials.

If you want to be a stickler, you should establish procedures to verify shareholder status for those who don't have credentials – and if you decide to exclude somebody on that basis, make sure you apply that consistently.

V. Annual Meetings – Conduct of the Meeting

106. Is a company allowed to establish rules for conducting the annual meeting that aren't in its bylaws?

Yes. Most bylaws don't contain any specific rules for conducting the annual meeting, but many contain language giving the chair the authority to establish rules of conduct for the meeting.

Regardless of whether they do or don't, the board of directors has broad authority to conduct the business and affairs of the corporation, and is well within its authority to adopt rules governing the conduct of a meeting – which is a best practice, even if the chair has authority under the bylaws.

107. Do "Robert's Rules of Order" apply?

Not unless your charter documents say that they do. In general, Roberts Rules are complex and inflexible, and are really ill-suited to a shareholders meeting.

They are designed for parliamentary bodies, and few corporate executives or their lawyers are familiar with them. I've seen other kinds of meetings get tied up in knots when somebody who does understand them shows up. Your rules should be simple, and they should be fair.

Rules of conduct often cover meeting room admission procedures, prohibition of recording or photography, the order of business to be addressed at the meeting, rules that will apply to speakers - such as who can speak, procedures for being recognized, limits on the number of individual questions and the time period that people may speak.

108. Is there a typical format for these meetings?

Yes, they are typically called to order, a statement indicating that a quorum is present is made, there may be introductions and a reminder of the rules that will govern the meeting, and then the meeting proceeds to each of the items on the agenda.

The inspectors of election report for each item on the agenda setting forth the preliminary vote tally is announced, and there's typically a statement that final information on the results will be announced following the meeting.

Once the matters on the agenda are addressed, it is customary to adjourn the meeting and then move on to a management presentation and Q&A.

This is a fairly typical format, but there are some variations. Some companies are much more formal in their approach – calling for motions and seconds before taking actions. Not everybody adjourns the meeting before the presentations and Q&A.

109. **Who participates in an annual meeting?**

The formal aspect of the meeting is usually a two person show – the board chair will typically chair the meeting, and will be assisted by the corporate secretary in addressing the formal aspects of the meeting – the corporate secretary will usually announce the information on each proposal provided by the inspectors of election, and whether or not it is sufficient for the proposal to pass.

As I mentioned previously, some companies will provide for motions and seconds in their scripts, and in these cases, there may be broader participation by management employees or directors who will chime in with a motion or a second.

After adjournment – which might happen within minutes of the meeting starting - participation may broaden to include several members of management and the board. The CEO and the CFO may run through management's presentation, and heads of business units and board committee chairs may be asked to address specific questions during any Q&A session.

110. <u>How should shareholder proposals from the floor be handled?</u>

If you have an advance notice bylaw that was not complied with, it may be appropriate to respond to the floor proposal with a statement to the effect that it has not been made in accordance with the company's bylaws and is out of order. Some companies point out the advance notice bylaw and its effect in their preliminary remarks.

If you don't have an advance notice bylaw, then the best practice is usually to bring the matter to a vote. Your proxy card will typically convey discretionary authority to vote as the proxy holders see fit with respect to any proposals that are brought before the meeting but are not known to the holders at the time.

Your discretionary authority will typically provide more than enough votes to defeat the proposal.

W. Annual Meetings - Handling the Media

111. Does the media have the right to attend a shareholders meeting?

No, but think long & hard before deciding to exclude them. You'll read about your decision in the paper, and it won't be with a positive spin.

112. What considerations go into a decision about whether to invite the media to the meeting?

This isn't often a tough call when times are good, but when the company is dealing with controversy, its first instinct is to prohibit the media from attending. That's usually a mistake – if there's controversy, this won't tamp it down, it will typically just throw fire on it. You end up looking like the Nixon White House – what are you trying to hide?

Also, media coverage -even if it has a negative spin – provides you a forum to get your side of the story out.

113. What preparations should be made if the media is going to be invited?

If you're going to actively encourage media attendance, then there are a bunch of things that you need to do in order to prepare.

These include getting the word out to media outlets about the meeting date, time and location well in advance, establishing and communicating any advance registration or other admission procedures that will apply to the media, putting together and sending out a press kit, deciding whether you're going to have a press room, seating arrangements, etc.

That's all logistic stuff, but you also need to establish rules for the media and let them know what they are – including whether and when photography and audio & videotaping is going to be allowed.

These are all great points if you're a giant company with a huge media following or if you just dumped 500 tons of radioactive waste into the Hudson, but for most companies what often happens is this: somebody from the paper or a local news crew shows up unannounced at the meeting.

You need to be prepared for this eventuality and think on your feet - "what if the media shows up?" is a contingency that you should prepare for, even if you aren't actively soliciting their attendance.

In most situations, the media doesn't act like they're the I-Team or Geraldo Rivera. Most commonly, I've seen the traditional news media approach a company representative to let them know they are in attendance before the meeting, and then comply with any instructions they are given.

I've also seen them approach corporate executives (usually the CEO) after the meeting for comment. The company's corporate communications person usually serves as the go-between for arranging these. You should always prep your CEO for encounters like these.

114. If members of the media are in attendance, do they have the right to ask questions?

They do not. And in practice, most companies don't permit them to ask questions publicly. But they sometimes are afforded opportunities to ask questions one-on-one with management. Depending on the circumstances, a company may want to consider a post-meeting press conference.

115. If you invite the media, can you still ban recording devices? Do you still have to worry about Reg FD?

Yes. The mere presence of the press isn't a free pass under Reg FD. Depending on the circumstances, you might be deemed to satisfy FD's requirement of effecting broad, non-exclusionary distribution of information to the public, but don't bank on it unless you've taken other steps - such as webcasting the meeting with appropriate notice.

X. Annual Meetings - Minutes

116. Since you report voting results on a Form 8-K anyway, why are minutes necessary?

Corporations exist only on paper. As with director actions, minutes are the formal record of actions taken at a shareholders meeting, and they're a statutory requirement in most states.

117. How detailed should the minutes be?

Annual meeting minutes typically aren't very detailed.

118. What matters should be addressed in the minutes?

You want to make sure that you've got all the important factual data about the meeting and cover the legal bases. Your minutes should set forth the date, time and location of the meeting. They should identify the persons who served as Chair & Secretary, the inspectors of election, the directors and officers in attendance, and the representatives of your auditor in attendance.

The minutes typically reference a certificate or report of the inspectors of election as to the presence of a quorum and the voting results, and an affidavit of mailing from the transfer agent with respect to the proxy statement. These are often attached as exhibits to the minutes.

The minutes recite the various proposals being acted upon, the names of director nominees and vote totals, the vote totals for other proposals, and note the meeting's adjournment.

The minutes should reference the fact that a management presentation and Q&A session was held after the meeting.

119. **Should the board approve minutes of the annual meeting?**

Yes. It's customary to circulate the minutes to the board and have them approve them at a board meeting.

120. **Should the minutes of the previous year's meeting be read at the annual meeting?**

There's no statutory requirement to do so in Delaware, and that's also the case in many other states – in fact, there's very little in the statute about minutes for shareholders meetings. The only requirement to keep minutes under the Delaware General Corporation Law (the "DGCL") comes from §142(a): "One of the officers shall have the duty to record the proceedings of the meetings of the stockholders and directors in a book to be kept for that purpose."

Some bylaw provisions setting forth annual meeting procedures include a requirement for the reading of the minutes, and many other companies start off the meeting with a call for a motion to waive the reading of the prior year's minutes.

Y. Annual Meetings - Postponement or Adjournment

121. Why would a company want to delay an annual meeting?

The most common reason is that you need more time to solicit votes or obtain a quorum. That can be because you've just disclosed new information that's material and you need to give the shareholders time to address it, or for other reasons, such as a short solicitation period or simply a desire to keep trying to get enough votes for a merger or other proposal to pass.

Of course, the natural disasters of the late summer and early fall of 2017 show that business in entire regions of the country can be disrupted for weeks at a time, so the physical inability to hold a meeting at the original time and location can sometimes also be a driving force behind a need to postpone.

122. Who has the authority to postpone or adjourn a meeting?

That's a good question - and one that often doesn't have a clear answer. If your bylaws provide that directors can postpone or adjourn a meeting, that's great. Otherwise, you'll find a statutory black hole or provisions that point to a need for shareholders to approve an adjournment.

Your proxy may include language giving the proxy holders authority to adjourn a meeting in order to solicit additional votes, but institutional investors aren't crazy about that and you often see them voting against something like this.

123. <u>What's the difference between postponement, adjournment & a recess?</u>

Postponing a meeting is a decision that's made by the board in advance of a meeting date.

Most lawyers are comfortable that a board has the authority to do this – assuming it called the meeting in the first place. The issue can get more complicated if a shareholder or group called the meeting. But, just because the "black letter" law suggests that the board has authority to do this, it doesn't mean that there aren't legal issues associated with such a decision.

Adjourning a meeting is an action taken after the meeting has been convened. The board or Chair's authority to do this is frequently less clear under statutory law or bylaw provisions. This is where that discretionary authority can come in handy.

A "recess" is a workaround developed by some very sharp lawyers to contend that a chair has the inherent authority to declare a recess – not adjourn the meeting, but continue it until a later time or date – regardless of statutory or bylaw provisions addressing adjournment.

When people think of a “recess,” they typically think of a brief period. But there’s no legal definition, and one company and its lawyers famously declared a “recess” that lasted several days in order to continue to solicit proxies.

124. What should companies consider before deciding to delay a shareholder meeting?

Many things – we’ve already touched on the whole topic of whether the board can do this without shareholder approval, and that’s a pretty fundamental issue. What do your bylaws say? Does your proxy convey authority to adjourn the meeting? Do you have the votes?

Beyond that, though, there are a lot of other issues to think about. These all come under the heading of “why are you doing this?” If you’ve got a quorum issue, your decision to adjourn or postpone a meeting is probably pretty defensible – but if you’re doing this because you don’t have the votes to approve a deal or a proposal that you want vote.

In the end, these issues are likely to be the same regardless of whether you formally adjourn the meeting or engage in semantic gymnastics and declare a “recess.”

125. **Does a decision to delay a meeting result in lawsuits? What are the legal issues that can arise?**

Delaware has a line of cases – *Blasius v. Atlas Industries* (Del. Ch.; 7/88) – that aren't used much, but stand for the proposition that unilateral board action designed to thwart the exercise of the shareholder franchise requires a "compelling justification."

That means no business judgment rule, and in at least one case involving delaying a meeting, the Delaware court has said that Blasius was implicated. See *State of Wisconsin Investment Board v. Peerless Systems Corp.* (Del. Ch.; 9/00), where the Delaware Court of Chancery required the board to show a "compelling justification" for adjourning the meeting - and warned companies to exercise "extreme caution" when attempting to alter the outcome of a shareholder vote.

Z. Proxy Advisors - Basics

126. Who are the major players?

"Proxy advisors" are members of a small cottage industry whose employees read most of the proxy statements & annual reports prepared by companies – and then write up analysis about them for each company and also make recommendations about how to vote for each item on a particular company's ballot for its upcoming annual shareholder meeting. Institutional investors will then pay those proxy advisors for that research – to help them vote their proxies at those companies in which they are shareholders.

In the US, the major players are ISS and Glass Lewis. ISS is by far the largest and most influential, with Glass Lewis a distant second. Others include Egan Jones & Siegal Marco Advisors. There are a bunch of others in other countries.

127. How influential are they?

That depends on who you ask, but their recommendations can clearly influence the outcome of a shareholder vote. Proxy advisors are influential because reliance on their recommendations is an easy way for institutional investors to fulfill their fiduciary obligations to their own investors.

Institutional investors simply don't have the time to make informed voting decisions on every stock in their portfolio, and in 2003, the SEC required them to start making disclosure about their votes. Institutions were concerned about their heightened profile of their vote, and noted that the SEC said that reliance on independent 3rd party advice might be a way to avoid violating their fiduciary duties when casting votes. For many institutional investors, this seemed like an affordable way to address their obligations.

Some institutional investors will follow the proxy advisor recommendations almost reflexively; others take the recommendations of ISS (in particular) into account when making their own voting decisions. Some institutional investors rely solely on their own internal staff for recommendations.

128. How do they solicit input on policies?

ISS has an annual process that's pretty transparent. ISS revises its proxy voting policies annually. ISS starts annual policy update process by asking investors – as well as companies and other interested parties - to weigh in on a policy survey regarding possible changes.

This kicks off sometime in the summer. It uses input from surveys of institutional investors and companies, industry group roundtables and ongoing feedback during the proxy season to develop draft policy updates on emerging governance issues each year.

The draft policy updates are then published for an open review and comment period before being finalized. Final policy updates are published each November for meetings held after February of the following year.

Glass Lewis also revises and publishes its proxy voting guidelines annually to reflect changes in best practices and new or emerging issues. The approach of Glass Lewis is different than ISS.

Glass Lewis will canvas its investor clients on a more informal basis during the year. And it will also receive company input when it conducts engagement with companies on a one-on-one basis. It relies on its Research Advisory Council in the corporate governance, accounting, financial transparency, and legal & regulatory arenas to guide the development of its voting policies & guidelines.

Updated guidelines are published each November for meetings held after January of the following year.

129. What information about their policies is publicly available?

ISS posts four sets of Policy Updates: US, Canada, Europe and Asia-Pacific. It also posts an

Executive Summary of the Key Updates and its Policy Development Process, as well as a set of FAQs. Although ISS makes three policy documents publicly available—annual policy updates, a summary set of the full policy guidelines and a "concise" guideline set (along with extensive FAQs about policy application), its detailed voting manual is not.

The detailed voting manual is made available solely to clients (e.g. institutional investors, proxy solicitors) and it provides a deeper dive with into the background of its policies, such as highlighting academic studies that may undergird a given policy.

Over the years, Glass Lewis has become more transparent with its policies. Until relatively recently, Glass Lewis wasn't transparent and even a summary of its policies wasn't publicly available. Now, it has a full set of guidelines for each of the markets it covers on GlassLewis.com.

130. Can you "engage" with proxy advisors?

Both Glass Lewis and ISS will engage with companies about their corporate governance practices, but each has its own process & timing for engagement. Not surprisingly (given that the proxy season is so busy), the best time for engagement is outside of the proxy season.

During the off-season, Glass Lewis is open to meeting with companies to clarify its operations, guidelines and perspectives, and to learn about the company. Glass Lewis also periodically hosts "Proxy Talk" conference calls with relevant parties (e.g., company representatives, dissidents, shareholder proposal proponents) that are accessible to its investor clients prior to publishing its research to obtain additional information that may be considered for its analysis.

Where it believes it will be productive, ISS will engage with companies, dissident shareholders and sponsors of shareholder proposals. Engagement may be initiated by ISS, companies or shareholders. In contested situations, ISS ordinarily engages with both sides.

Glass Lewis won't engage with companies on specific proxy proposals after the company's proxy statement has been filed except when its analysts require clarification on a particular issue. For non-contentious situations, ISS may engage during that time at the proxy analyst's discretion - generally only to clarify points on which companies have questions about ISS' analysis.

Both ISS and Glass Lewis will use only publicly available information to develop their analyses and recommendations.

AA. Proxy Advisors – Reports & Recommendations

131. Do proxy advisors provide companies with a draft of their voting reports?

"Voting reports" are reports with specific analysis about a particular company. ISS provides S&P 500 companies with draft copies of their voting reports so they have an opportunity to review the drafts and correct any errors. They typically get this draft report about 24-48 hours before ISS makes a company's report available to its investor clients.

ISS does this because these large companies are widely held and it wants to spare itself the embarrassment of issuing a subsequent alert to make a correction.

Glass Lewis allows companies to review an Issuer Data Report (IDR) comprising the key data points it uses in developing its report on the company's annual meeting – but the IDR doesn't have Glass Lewis' analysis or voting recommendations. Glass Lewis will only issue IDRs for companies that have released all proxy materials no less than 30 days before the annual meeting date.

ISS voting reports aren't publicly available – they are only available for purchase with an exception that ISS provides a final voting report to any company it covers if they sign up to receive them.

Glass Lewis charges everybody – even the company that's the subject of the report, and they aren't cheap.

132. Can companies correct information in those reports?

Yes, but unless you're in the S&P 500, you won't be able to do that until after the report has been issued. The limited access to these reports is one of the things that companies find most frustrating about dealing with proxy advisors.

133. Can companies share those reports with their own advisors?

No, they cannot – another thing that drives companies and their advisors crazy. You can sometimes get access to them, but there are hoops to jump through and fees to be paid.

134. How often do proxy advisors side with shareholder proposal proponents?

I think the last information I saw put it at about 80% on standard governance stuff, but it varies from year-to-year. In 2016, ISS supported nearly all proxy access proposals, 3/4ths of independent chair proposals, 2/3rds of ESG proposals & 2/3rds of compensation proposals. So, they clearly tilt toward the shareholder side of things, but they aren't monolithic.

135. What factors can lead to an "against/withhold" recommendation on a director?

There are a wide variety of perceived failings that can lead to a withhold recommendation. By far, the largest source of negative recommendations are based on independence issues (non-independent non-executive directors on key committees or failure to maintain a majority independent board). Compensation issues loom large too.

Governance decisions can also be triggers, such as taking unilateral action that reduces shareholder rights (or failing to put pre-IPO restrictive provisions to a shareholder vote), absence of a formal nominating committee, pledging of shares by executives (ISS sees this as a failure of risk oversight), failing to implement a successful shareholder proposal, and poor attendance.

BB. Proxy Access

136. Why do shareholders want companies to adopt "proxy access" bylaws?

Traditionally, if a shareholder wanted to nominate a candidate - or a slate of candidates - for election as directors, they had to put together their own proxy materials and conduct a proxy fight. That's expensive & cumbersome.

Proxy access bylaws give investors – the ones who can jump through the hoops set forth in the company's bylaw provisions - the ability to include their nominees along with management's nominees in the company's proxy statement.

137. How common are proxy access bylaws?

Proxy access bylaws have become very common, particularly among large cap companies. More than 60% of the S&P 500 have proxy access bylaws.

The growth in these bylaws has been explosive – two companies adopted proxy access bylaws in 2013, five the following year, and then BOOM! From roughly the end of the 2016 proxy season through the bulk of the 2017 proxy season, an additional 175 companies have adopted proxy access bylaws (or charter provisions), bringing the total number to more than 425.

There's a reason that things started to build around 2013. Rule 14a-11, the SEC's proxy access rule, originally intended to take effect in November 2010, was stayed and ultimately vacated by the DC Circuit in July 2011.

When it adopted proxy access, the SEC also amended Rule 14a-8 to permit shareholder proposals regarding proxy access, and that was not affected by the DC Circuit decision. After the SEC's stay on that rule expired in 2011, proxy access shareholder proposals started to trickle in, and then became a flood.

138. Have the terms of these bylaws become standardized?

Yes, at least for the main features. The basic requirements for proxy access bylaws are now pretty standardized: you've got to own at least 3% of the company's shares for at least 3 years, and you can satisfy that requirement by aggregating the ownership of up to 20 shareholders, and candidates for up to 20% of board seats can be nominated through proxy access (with a minimum of two nominees).

There's less uniformity in some other areas, but most bylaws require some minimum level of support for a nominee (15-20%) to re-nominate that person. Most bylaws also either count directors recently elected through the access process toward the maximum number of nominees allowed in a particular year – assuming the board re-nominates those people – or impose a cooling off period on further nominations from the shareholder whose candidate was elected.

Most bylaws also cut off proxy access in the event of proxy fight or reduce the number of access nominees for that annual meeting by the number of advance notice nominees submitted for the same meeting.

139. **If a company has a proxy access bylaw, is that typically the only way for a shareholder to nominate a director?**

No, but it's the only way to get on the company's proxy statement.

If you want to nominate somebody and solicit your own proxies – which is how it's traditionally been done and how it is still done in practice – you just need to comply with whatever requirements may be imposed by the company's charter documents on nominations of directors.

These requirements can be pretty elaborate if a company has adopted an advance notice bylaw.

140. What are "fix it" proposals - and how has the SEC responded to company requests to exclude them?

"Fix-it" proposals are shareholder proposals submitted for the purpose of modifying the provisions of a previously adopted proxy access bylaw. Most of the fix-it proposals this year related to increasing the limit on the size of the group that could be aggregated for purposes of satisfying the 3% threshold. 33 companies during the 2017 proxy season sought to exclude these proposals.

The vast majority were successful - 31 persuaded the Staff that the proposals should be excluded on the basis of "substantial implementation" under Rule 14a-8(i)(10), but it's really an exercise in reading tea leaves to figure out what distinguished those companies that were successful in persuading the Staff that fix-it proposals could be excluded from those that were unsuccessful.

The basic argument that companies made was that given their shareholder base, going from 20 to, say, 50 shareholders wouldn't move the needle in terms of the ability of shareholders to nominate a candidate. When it excluded proposals, the Corp Fin Staff found that the company's "policies, practices and procedures compare favorably with the guidelines of the proposal and that [the company] has, therefore, substantially implemented the proposal."

The SEC Staff denied no-action relief to two companies under substantially similar circumstances when it was "unable to conclude that [the company] has met its burden of establishing that it may exclude the proposal under rule 14a-8(i)(10)."

Sidley & Austin wrote a memo saying that the reason those companies were denied relief appears to be that their request letters failed to include specific information regarding the ownership of the company's institutional holders—as opposed to all holders or large holders—when arguing that the existing proxy access bylaw already provides a meaningful proxy access right.

Of the 31 companies that were successful in obtaining no-action relief, four were initially denied relief and then submitted requests for reconsideration with details about institutional ownership, which were granted by the SEC Staff.

Why does this matter? Nobody's really sure – and because of the nature of the no-action letter process, the Staff doesn't really lay out its reasoning.

CC. Proxy Contests

141. What's the SEC Staff's role in a proxy contest?

The Corp Fin Staff does play a role. In fact, they are never more like a referee than they are for proxy contests. Every scrap of paper that flies back & forth from the insurgents and the company gets filed with the SEC.

They review each of them. And they frequently have fairly extensive comments on it - usually prefaced with a statement like "Each statement or assertion of opinion or belief must be clearly characterized as such, and a reasonable factual basis must exist for each such opinion or belief. Support for opinions or beliefs should be self-evident, disclosed in the proxy statement or provided to the staff on a supplemental basis" – then they drill down to statements that concern them.

142. What communications have to be filed with the SEC?

Any written material that can be characterized as "soliciting material" needs to be filed with the SEC. Rule 14a-1 defines solicitation very broadly, and so really anything you send to shareholders (and any scripts that you prepare for calls with shareholders), and written materials you send to proxy advisors, and any ads you take out, and anything you post on social media tweets you write or third-party tweets you retweet – all of this stuff can be regarded as soliciting material and you have to file it.

This applies to insurgents too. One example of a communication like this that may only apply to insurgents is if the insurgents want to call a special meeting and do a mailing to shareholders asking for them to join in the call (which is often necessary to round up enough percentages), that's soliciting material and has to be filed.

Rule 14a-12 allows you to make communications that fall under the broad definition of solicitation before you file a proxy statement, but if you do, there are specific filing and legend requirements that you need to address. You also don't have a lot of time to make a filing – any soliciting material has to be filed no later than the day you first disseminate it.

143. What's a "fight letter"?

A "fight letter" is a tool for marketing your position in a proxy contest to investors – primarily, retail investors. You're going to be meeting one-on-one with your major institutional investors, but it's not physically possible to meet with most of the people on the retail side.

There are usually a number of these issued by each side during the course of the fight, and they're kind of fun to write.

They aren't real long – three or four pages maybe. The first one lays out the main arguments in support of your position and against the bad guys' position. These are followed up by more letters touching on specific themes that your side thinks are its real winners.

Sometimes, your first fight letter is written in response to a communication from the insurgents, in which case you're a little bit on your heels, because you're reacting to what they said. While responding to misleading statements in their materials is usually necessary, most of your time should be spent on presenting your case to investors.

It's misleading to call these "letters" - they may include letters, but are often accompanied by a slide deck or other materials designed to highlight the salient points supporting your side's arguments or attacking the other side. The company will likely establish a dedicated area on its website for these materials and the insurgents will invariably have a much cooler website of their own for theirs.

And again, all of this stuff is getting filed and reviewed by the Staff.

144. When do the proxy advisors get involved?

ISS will wait to engage with either side until everything's definitive. They won't engage if only preliminary proxy materials are filed with the SEC.

ISS doesn't have a policy for proxy contests; it focuses on two things – and puts the burden on the insurgents to make a case:

- Have the insurgents made a compelling case that change is needed?
- If they have, which nominees are most likely to effect that change?

ISS will meet with both sides, but the insurgents go first and management is expected to respond to their arguments. These meetings typically take place around 20 days in advance of the meeting.

145. Do most proxy contests seek to replace the entire board?

No, that's pretty unusual these days. Proxy advisors aren't crazy about wholesale replacement of the board. And institutional investors are more likely to support adding a couple of candidates to "shake things up" in the boardroom than they are to a proposal that would oust the entire board.

DD. Shareholder Proposals

146. What is a "shareholder proposal"? What rights do shareholders have to include proposals in a company's proxy statement?

A "shareholder proposal" is a matter that an individual shareholder of the company wants to submit to a vote at an annual meeting. A SEC rule has long provided a route for shareholders to include a proposal in management's proxy statement.

That process is governed by Rule 14a-8. The rule's written in a plain English "Q&A" format, and lays out procedural and substantive requirements that a shareholder must meet in order to have their proposal included in the proxy statement.

If shareholders don't meet these requirements, companies can seek to have their proposals excluded from their proxy materials. They notify the Corp Fin Staff of their intent to exclude a proposal – through a "no-action letter request" - and send a copy of that request to the proponent.

The Staff then considers the request—along with any rebuttal provided by the proponents—and issues a response indicating its views with respect to the company's intention to omit the proposal.

147. How often do companies receive shareholder proposals?

Large companies can expect them almost every year – frequently, they'll receive multiple proposals. Some smaller companies get them – some don't.

I had a client that entered the S&P 500 a few years ago, and they went from getting one proposal every 3-4 years to getting a couple every single year. It just goes with the territory.

148. How do companies - and proponents - interact on a proposal?

There is usually a fair amount of interaction. Depending on the nature of the proposal and who it comes from, the company may negotiate to make governance changes or take other actions in response to the proposal that satisfy the proponent and results in the proposal being withdrawn.

Even if the company determines to fight a proposal (through the Corp Fin Staff's no-action letter process), it may still continue to negotiate with the proponent during that process.

149. On what basis can a company exclude a proposal?

There are both procedural and substantive bases that would permit a company to exclude a shareholder proposal. These substantive bases – laid out in Rule 14a-8 - include:

1. The proposal isn't a proper subject for action by shareholders under the laws of the jurisdiction of the company's organization;
2. If implemented, the proposal would cause the company to violate any state, federal or foreign law to which it is subject;
3. The proposal is contrary to any of the SEC's proxy rules, including Rule 14a-9;
4. It involves redress of a personal claim or grievance against the company or any other person or involves a matter personal to the proponent;
5. The proposal relates to operations that account for less than 5% of the company's total assets at the end of its most recent fiscal year, and for less than 5% of its net earnings and gross sales for its most recent fiscal year, and is not otherwise significantly related to the company's business;

6. The company lacks the power or authority to implement the proposal;
7. The proposal involves a matter relating to the company's ordinary business operations;
8. The proposal involves election for membership on the company's board of directors or analogous governing body;
9. The proposal directly conflicts with one of the company's own proposals to be submitted to shareholders at the same meeting;
10. The company has already substantially implemented the proposal.

Procedural requirements in Rule 14a-8 include things like meeting minimum ownership requirements – you have to have held at least $2,000 worth of the company's stock (or 1% of the shares eligible to vote, whichever figure is smaller) continuously for at least one year before the date the proposal is submitted to the company.

In addition, you must hold the stock through the date of the annual meeting and agree to present (or have a qualified representative present) the proposal at the meeting. You also have to meet the deadline for submitting a proposal – typically 120 calendar days before the date of the company's proxy statement released to shareholders in connection with the previous year's annual meeting.

If you want to ding somebody on procedural grounds, then you need to tell them what they did wrong within 14 days of receiving the proposal, and then they have 14 days to fix it.

By the way, that's kind of a theme here, even on some of the substantive grounds for exclusion, the Corp Fin Staff will give shareholders the ability to modify their proposal to address the problems identified in the no-action process.

150. What's the SEC Staff's role in the process?

Rule 14a-8 gives the Corp Fin Staff the role of arbiter – if you want to exclude, you typically need to go through the no-action process.

What they tell you is non-binding, but it is usually treated as definitive as a practical matter. You can litigate this if you want - and a couple of companies have, but not many.

EE. Shareholder Activism

151. Who are the activists - and what are their objectives?

You can slice & dice activism in a number of ways. For example, many different types of investors are activists when it comes to governance issues, executive pay, ESG (stands for "environmental, social & governance") and other oversight issues. These include individual investors, public or labor pension funds, religious groups or other coalitions. Many of these investors use the shareholder proposal process under Rule 14a-8 as their primary engagement tool.

Activist hedge funds are different. We do an annual DealLawyers.com webcast entitled "Activists Profiles & Playbooks" that gives you a good overview of who the activist funds are and how they approach potential opportunities.

Some are household names – Icahn Associates, Pershing Square, Trian, Jana Partners – while you've never heard of many of the others. More than 100 hedge funds currently engaged in frequent activism & over 300 others that have launched activism campaigns in recent years – and they continue to attract interest from major institutional investors.

Activist hedge funds are very different in their approaches, but they typically have one thing in common

– most of them pursue what are referred to as "event driven" investment strategies. That is, their objective most frequently is to point the company toward a particular transaction that will result in a superior return on their investment.

This can be a sale transaction, divestitures, a leveraged dividend or stock repurchase or other liquidity event. You may see them use the shareholder proposal process, but their proposals usually focus on enhancing shareholder value and are just one component of a broader campaign.

152. <u>What makes a company an activist target?</u>

It's funny, there's a great quote from Carl Icahn where he supposedly said "they used to call me a raider, now I'm an activist." Many of the same factors that led a company to be a potential target for a hostile takeover back in the day may make it attractive to activists now.

These guys are looking for a deal, so they want a bankable company – profitable companies that are undervalued in the stock market are attractive targets, particularly if they have strong cash flows. For the same reason, companies sitting on a stockpile of cash are attractive.

Companies with underperforming businesses or whose profile suggests that they might be able to create more value for shareholders by pursuing an alternative to their existing strategies are also on the radar.

Companies that underperform and are outliers when it comes to governance are also very attractive – governance is a wedge that activists can use to push open the door to a broader agenda.

Any company with a large institutional ownership base is a potential target.

153. How should a company respond to an overture from an activist?

The first thing you should remember is that by the time you hear from them, they've already spoken with your major institutional investors. They've usually accompanied their discussions with a "white paper" or some other well-researched documentation supporting their views.

In most cases, that means it's smart to meet with the activist and hear its criticisms and proposals. This isn't an opportunity to fight, but to listen and learn. Like I said, your institutional investors have already heard the pitch.

Don't expect the activist to limit its contact to management – expect the activist to reach out to individual directors. You need to prepare your board for the possibility of activism.

The worst time to respond to the threat of activism is when an activist shows up on your doorstep. Well before this, you should have worked to engage your board on strategic matters – look at alternatives to your strategic plan, get updates from bankers on M&A and other transactional trends in your industry, know where you stand in comparison to your peers and why something that works for them might not work for you.

Engage with your major shareholders – make sure they understand why you're pursuing the strategy that you're pursuing. Your best defense when an activist comes knocking is often to be in a position to say "you know, we thought of that and the board considered it, and here's why we didn't think it made sense for our company."

154. How do institutional investors respond to activists?

Increasingly, they hear them out. Everybody is seeking "alpha" - investment returns that beat the market - and in a market that's been as strong as this one has been over the past decade, that's hard to find.

Activists promise a path to above market returns, and that's a pitch that's going to get listened to by institutional investors. Institutions know that when activists show up, there's a short-term pop in the stock price and that it's often followed by some sort of liquidity event at a premium.

That being said, a lot of major institutional investors are increasingly skeptical of activists and the short-term approach that their strategies often embody, and it is worth the company's time to engage with these investors. BlackRock, Vanguard & State Street often hold the outcome of a proxy contest in their hands.

They aren't necessarily swayed by ISS, and when a company's management and directors can present a compelling case for long-term value creation associated with their strategies, these investors will often be supportive even in the face of activism.

155. Are antitakeover devices useful in dealing with an activist?

Some can be in the event of a proxy contest, but the game is very different from what those defenses were put in place to protect against, so if your reaction to activism is to adopt a bunch of new antitakeover devices, then you're fighting the last war.

These guys aren't raiders – they typically aren't looking to acquire a company in a hostile deal, but to have the company enter into a transaction that gives them the return they're looking for. They often own relatively small stakes in the company.

I do think advance notice bylaws are very important in order to provide sufficient time to address a potential proxy contest with an activist.

FF. Exchange Act Reports – Basics

156. What is a proxy statement?

When a company holds a shareholders meeting, it needs to obtain votes from hundreds, or sometimes thousands, of individual shareholders. Those people could theoretically all show up at the meeting and vote in person, but life doesn't work like that. Very few show up at the actual shareholders meeting.

So, what companies do is solicit proxies from their shareholders. Those proxies authorize the holders named in the proxy card to vote in accordance with the instructions provided by the shareholder from whom the proxy is solicited. (Technically speaking, many of these "proxy cards" are actually "voting instruction forms" – this is a complex topic. Learn more in our "Proxy Card/Voting Instruction Form Handbook" posted on TheCorporateCounsel.net.)

The Exchange Act and the SEC's proxy rules require the filing of a disclosure document known as a proxy statement before any proxies can be solicited. It contains detailed information about the matters to be acted upon, information about beneficial ownership of shares, interests of related parties, etc.

If directors are going to be elected, it will contain information about each nominee and other directors, executive compensation, governance matters, etc. If a deal is being voted on, there will likely be financial information included as well.

157. What is a 10-K (and glossy annual report)?

A 10-K is an annual report that's required to be filed with the SEC under the Exchange Act. It includes a description of the business, MD&A, three years of financial statements, exhibits, officer certifications as to disclosure controls and procedures, internal control over financial reporting and the accuracy of the report and the financial information included in it.

In addition, information about directors and executive officers, executive compensation, compensation plans, change in control and termination payments, beneficial ownership of shares and other matters are required, but are typically incorporated by reference from the proxy statement (assuming you can get that on file within 120 days of the end of your fiscal year).

Companies are required to send annual reports to their shareholders when they hold annual meetings. This report in its historically traditional form is commonly referred to as the "glossy" annual report. However, about 50% of companies now are using a "10-K wrap" or just a 10-K to meet this obligation. The term "glossy" only refers to the traditional format of the report (which was glossy) - it's not what many companies are doing nowadays.

This annual report is different from the annual report on Form 10-K - which is required to be filed with the SEC - but is not required to be mailed to shareholders. (However, one document may in fact satisfy both requirements.)

Learn more in our "Form 10-K Handbook" and "Annual Report & 10-K Wrap Handbook" posted on TheCorporateCounsel.net.

158. What is a 10-Q?

A 10-Q is a quarterly report that companies are required to file with the SEC after each of the first three quarters of their fiscal years. The 10-Q includes financial statements (unaudited) for the quarter and year to date, together with comparable quarterly data for the prior fiscal year.

It will also have an MD&A section, CEO/CFO certifications and exhibits, and it may also contain other information, such as information about material litigation.

159. What is an 8-K?

An 8-K is a current report that companies must file with the SEC upon the occurrence of specific events.

Events that prompt an 8-K filing include entry into or termination of a material agreement, bankruptcy, incurrence of certain financial obligations and charges, completion of certain acquisitions or divestitures, changes in charter documents, changes in directors or management, violations of listing standards, changes in accountants, results of shareholder voting, exempt issuances of securities.

Companies also have to "furnish" – not file – their earnings releases and may also furnish information on Form 8-K to satisfy their FD disclosure obligations. This is a legal distinction as these "furnished" 8-Ks are still filed on the SEC's Edgar.

160. How do you figure out what belongs in them? What are Regulations S-K & S-X and how do they relate to the form?

Each form is, well, *a form* – it has specific instructions that refer you to particular line items of Regulation S-K or S-X for the specific disclosures that must be included in your filing.

Reg S-K deals with narrative disclosures – its line items cover all of the non-financial disclosure requirements in the filings, while Reg S-X addresses the financial statements and pro forma information that are required in a particular filing.

But, it's important to keep in mind that these aren't "fill-in-the-blank" forms. You always need to keep in mind Rule 12b-20, which says that: "In addition to the information expressly required to be included in a statement or report, there shall be added such further material information, if any, as may be necessary to make the required statements, in the light of the circumstances under which they are made not misleading."

GG. SEC Filings - Basics

161. What is "Edgar"?

Edgar is an acronym for the SEC's "Electronic Data Gathering, Analysis and Retrieval" system. It's the SEC's electronic filing system – and virtually all SEC filings must be made electronically now. This Edgar database is freely available on the SEC's website.

162. What are the deadlines for SEC filings?

For companies, the answer for Form 10-K and Form 10-Q depends on whether or not they are "non-accelerated filers," "accelerated filers" or "large accelerated filers."

Category of Filer	Deadlines for Filing Periodic Reports	
	Form 10-K Deadline	Form 10-Q Deadline
Large Accelerated Filer ($700MM or more)	60 days	40 days
Accelerated Filer ($75MM or more and less than $700MM)	75 days	40 days
Non-accelerated Filer (less than $75MM)	90 days	45 days

Accelerated filers typically are companies that have a public float of at least $75 million. Large accelerated filers include companies with a public float of $700 million or more, and non-accelerated filers are the little guys.

Proxy statements don't technically have a deadline – but if you want to incorporate by reference the compensation & other disclosures into your 10-K, you need to have the definitive proxy statement on file 120 days after the end of your fiscal year.

So in reality, proxy statements do have a deadline. In fact, you may need to file a "preliminary" proxy statement if you have certain matters on the agenda for the shareholder meeting that can make the filing of your proxy statement a difficult one (see our "Preliminary Proxy Statements Handbook" on TheCorporateCounsel.net).

Or the use of notice & access (ie. e-proxy) or the resolution of a no-action letter request over shareholder proposals that may need to be included in the proxy can throw a wrench into your mailing schedule too. In many cases, your "Time & Responsibility Schedule" can fall to pieces when it comes to filing your proxy statement because there will be a number of factors beyond your control.

Form 8-Ks are typically due 4 business days after the triggering event – no matter what filer category you fall into - although financial statements for an acquisition can be deferred for up to 75 days.

Check out our "Disclosure Deadlines Handbook" posted on TheCorporateCounsel.net for more information.

163. Who makes the filing?

Some larger companies do it themselves, but because the document has to be specially formatted for filing ("Edgarized"), many companies outsource the process to financial printers or other third-party providers.

Somebody from the company always pushes the button and authorizes the filing. This is usually someone pretty high up in the law department or in the financial reporting area. Making an SEC filing is serious business.

164. What can I do if there is a mistake in making a filing?

It depends on the nature of the mistake. If it's a typographical error that doesn't substantively impact disclosure, the answer frequently is to not do anything. If there's a material misstatement or omission, however, the filing should promptly be amended to address it.

165. What if I have to amend a filing?

All amendments to Form 10-K or 10-Q must be filed on Form 10-K/A or a Form 10-Q/A. Amendments must set forth the complete text of each Item amended and must be signed by a duly authorized officer of the company.

An amendment to any report required to be accompanied by CEO/CFO certifications must include new certifications by those officers. See Exchange Act Rule 12b-15.

A Form 8-K is also amended by filing a Form 8-K/A.

The big question is whether companies should update the disclosure when they amend their Form10-K or 10-Q. Although we can't think of SEC Staff authority for the belief, many practitioners argue that an amended filing speaks as of the date of the original filing.

The reason is to avoid the implication that the entire filing is being updated thru the date of the amendment. It's partly for clarification, but mainly to limit potential liability to a plaintiff who might allege that the 10-K/A was materially misleading because it suggested that everything in the original 10-K had been brought current when in fact parts had become stale.

Proxy statements are a little more complicated – particularly if they've already been mailed. The issue there is whether to amend or supplement a proxy that's in need of revision.

Materiality is the key factor in deciding whether to supplement or amend. If there's a material error in the proxy, you should amend it or file a revised proxy statement. New or additional information could be provided through either an amendment or a supplement, depending on how important it is.

If a company needs to make a material change to a "non-routine" proposal, which originally necessitated a preliminary proxy statement, then it needs to decide if the 10-day wait period for preliminary proxy statements recommences.

The SEC provides in its rules that filing revised material does not recommence the 10-day time period, unless the revised material contains material revisions or material new proposal(s) that constitute a fundamental change in the proxy material.

HH. Exchange Act Filing Deadlines

166. How do you determine whether a day is a "business day"? Does it depend on whether the markets are open?

For purposes of the Form 8-K deadline, the term "business day" means any day the SEC is open for business. A list of federal holidays for the applicable year can be found on the SEC's website, under "Information for Edgar Filers." Sometimes a holiday falls on a weekend and the government is closed on Monday instead—when that happens, the Monday is not considered a business day.

In addition, there are a host of other circumstances that crop up irregularly that may—or may not—be considered a business day, such as presidential inaugurations (likely a business day) and snowstorms that close the federal government in DC (these still are business days). A quick look online (or on our blog on TheCorporateCounsel.net) will usually reveal whether the SEC is considered "open for business."

167. When does the "4-business day" clock start running for a Form 8-K filing?

Because the deadline is defined as four business days "after" the triggering event, the count begins the day after the triggering event takes place. For example, if the triggering event occurs on a Tuesday, Day One would be Wednesday, and the fourth business day (and the Form 8-K deadline) would be the following Monday. See Exchange Act Rule 0-3.

Similarly, if a triggering event occurs on a Tuesday, and the following Monday is a federal holiday, then the Form 8-K would be due on the following Tuesday.

Trust me, now that you know this, you will still count business days on your fingers your entire career.

168. Are all 8-Ks due within 4 business days?

No. As a practical matter, for example, Item 2.02 requires you to furnish a Form 8-K containing information about a completed quarter if you disclose that publicly. There's an exemption that applies to communications within 48 hours of filing that document that's basically intended to cover any additional information you communicate through a conference call.

But you have to have that 2.02 filing done in advance in order to take advantage of it. What that means as a practical matter is that people file their earnings release the same day they issue it, so that they can fit their conference call in within the exemption.

Also, there are certain amendments to Form 8-K that are due in less than 4 business days. For example, if you're changing accountants, you need to file any letter that you receive from your former auditor saying whether or not it agrees with your Form 8-K disclosure within 2 business days of receipt. Similarly, if a director resigns due to a disagreement, the director has to be provided with the 8-K filing and if the director wants to furnish a letter stating whether they agrees or disagrees with the disclosure, then you've got 2 days to amend the 8-K to disclose that.

If you need acquired company financial statements to make an 8-k filing, you have 71 days after you file your initial Form 8-K reporting the closing under Item 2.01 to get those on file.

169. Can you get an extension of the due date for an SEC filing?

You can get an up to 15-day extension for a late 10-K and a 5-day extension for a late 10-Q by filing a Form 12b-25 no later than the day after the original filing is due.

A Form 12b-25 is a disclosure document, and does require disclosure of as much information about the quarter as can be provided, as well as a statement about any material changes from prior periods. There's no extension for a late 8-K.

170. The SEC's "Edgar" accepts filings until 10 pm Eastern. So long as I file a report that's due on a particular date by then, is that timely?

Nope. You've got to get your reports on file by 5:30 pm Eastern in order to be regarded as having filed them on that particular date. Filings after that time will be given the next day as a filing date.

II. Accelerated v. Non-Accelerated Filer Status

171. What are the "categories" of filers?

Non-accelerated filers, accelerated filers and large accelerated filers. Non-accelerated filers are those companies with less than $75 million in public float.

Accelerated filers are companies that have a public float of at least $75 million, that have been subject to the Exchange Act's reporting requirements for at least 12 calendar months, that previously have filed at least one annual report, and that are not eligible to file their quarterly and annual reports on Forms 10-Q and 10-K using scaled disclosure requirements, and Large accelerated filers are those with more than $700 million in public float.

172. What are the filing deadlines for each category of filers?

Everybody has the same 8-K deadlines. Large accelerated filers include companies with a public float of $700 million or more.

Category of Filer	Revised Deadlines for Filing Periodic Reports	
	Form 10-K Deadline	Form 10-Q Deadline

Large Accelerated Filer ($700MM or more)	60 days	40 days
Accelerated Filer ($75MM or more and less than $700MM)	75 days	40 days
Non-accelerated Filer (less than $75MM)	90 days	45 days

173. When - and how - do you determine what category you're in?

Your filer category for the next fiscal year is determined by reference to your public float calculated as of the last business day of your most recently completed second fiscal quarter.

174. When will a change in your filer status become effective?

Even though you look to your public float at the end of your fiscal second quarter, your filer status won't change until the end of your fiscal year.

If your filer status does change, then you have to file on the new schedule commencing with your 10-K for the most recently completed fiscal year - and all subsequent quarterly & annual reports - by the deadline for your new status.

175. Can you be both a smaller reporting company and an accelerated filer?

Yes, you can. Here's how – let's say that you had a company with a public float of $80 million as of the last day of its fiscal quarter during 2016. For 2017, that company would be an accelerated filer.

If as of the last day of the company's second fiscal quarter of 2017, its public float dropped to $70 million, it would satisfy the test for being treated as a smaller reporting company for fiscal 2018, because it met the less than $75 million float threshold.

However, like Al Pacino in "Godfather III," when it comes to being an accelerated filer, "every time I try to get out, they pull me back in!"

You see, once a company becomes an accelerated filer, it will remain one until the market value of common equity held by non-affiliates drops below $50 million, as of the last business day of its most recently completed second fiscal quarter. Since the company in this example still has a public float of $70 million, it is still required to report on an accelerated basis. So, that's how this company ends up being both a smaller reporting company and an accelerated filer for 2018.

JJ. CEO & CFO Certifications

176. Where do the CEO & CFO certification requirements come from?

They come from Section 302 and Section 906 of the Sarbanes-Oxley Act. This 2002 law obligates the CEO and CFO of each public company to certify quarterly and annual reports filed with the SEC.

There are two required certifications:

– As mandated by Section 302 of Sarbanes-Oxley, the SEC adopted rules in 2002 requiring that the principal executive officer and principal financial officer of all reporting companies certify each annual and quarterly report filed under Exchange Act Section 13(a) or 15(d).

– Section 906 also requires a principal executive officer and principal financial officer certification. The Section 906 certification requirement was enacted under the U.S. criminal laws—so this certification is regulated by the Department of Justice—not the SEC directly.

The DOJ has not issued any rules or guidance on this certification, but Section 906 sets forth what is required.

The legislative purpose behind Sections 302 and 906 was to enhance investor confidence in the quality and reliability of a company's periodic reports by prompting

CEOs and CFOs to take a more proactive role in the processes for public disclosures of financial and other information.

Remember, this all came about in the wake of Enron's collapse in 2001, where one of the defenses that Enron's CEO put forward was that he was "out of the loop" on the company's financial shenanigans. Congress wanted to prevent that – they wanted the CEO and CFO's fingerprints all over the company's public disclosures. So, they forced them to clearly assume individual responsibility for the accuracy and completeness of periodic report disclosures.

When you read the text of the certifications with this in mind, they're easier to understand. The first thing they ask is for the officers to confirm that they've read the report, and to the best of their knowledge, it doesn't contain any material misstatements or omissions and that the financial statements fairly present its results.

Then, it gets down into the weeds – the officers have to take ownership for the process by which the filing is created – they have to acknowledge their responsibility for the company's disclosure controls & procedures and internal control over financial reporting, and they have to their conclusions about the effectiveness of those controls & disclose any material changes in internal control that took place during a quarter.

177. <u>Why are there two separate types of certifications? Can they be combined into a single form?</u>

I think the answer is that Sarbanes-Oxley was passed in a rush – just a matter of days - and the two overlapping requirements were never harmonized. Nobody really knows if this is what Congress intended, but it is what it is.

Even though the Sections 302 and 906 certifications have some overlap, they are distinct and have different applications and unique disclosure requirements. You can't combine the two.

178. <u>Are the certifications required to be filed with every SEC filing?</u>

No. The Section 302 certification requirement applies to each annual and quarterly report filed with the SEC—including Form 10-K, Form 10-Q, Form 20-F and Form 40-F. In addition, the requirement covers amendments to—and transition reports on—any of these reports. However, the SEC specifically excluded Form 11-K from the requirement even though it is an annual report.

The Section 302 certification requirement doesn't apply to current reports—including Forms 8-K or proxy statements, Regardless, disclosure controls and procedures are required to be designed, maintained and evaluated to ensure full and timely disclosure in current reports as well as definitive proxy materials and information statements (i.e., all required Exchange Act disclosures—whatever the document), even though there is no specific certification requirement relating to those forms.

Any amendment to a periodic report also has to contain a Section 302 certification. That isn't the case for the Section 906 certification – that only applies to reports containing financial statements, so if your amendment doesn't include financial statements, you don't have to include that certification.

179. What happens if a CEO or CFO resigns - or is terminated? Who signs the certifications?

The certifications are signed by whoever is fulfilling that role at the time the filing is due.

There's no slack cut here – the certifications have to be signed by the people holding the positions (function over title), even if they just joined the company – and even if the two people who held the titles previously are still at the company in a different capacity. See our "CEO/CFO Certifications Handbook" posted on TheCorporateCounsel.net.

180. What are the consequences if your filing doesn't include the required certifications?

Well, if you neglect to include one entirely, your filing is deficient – so if you don't amend it before the due date, you are delinquent and you've blown S-3 eligibility.

When you amend in this situation, you have re-file the entire document, not just the certifications.

Errors in the certifications don't have the same result, but the Corp Fin Staff scrubs these pretty closely and if you identify the wrong period, you fail to include a conformed signature, you don't date it, or the wrong people sign it, then you're always going to have to amend it.

KK. 8-K Exhibits

181. Are exhibits required to be filed with a Form 8-K?

Exhibits typically are not required to be filed with a Form 8-K, but they often are – especially in M&A settings. If you're doing a deal, investors want to see these documents and it's helpful to have their terms (including fiduciary outs, go-shops & no-shops) publicly available as soon as possible.

That means you'll frequently see merger agreements filed as exhibits to Item 1.01 8-Ks, even though you could technically wait until the next periodic report.

There are exceptions to the general rule that exhibits aren't required. For example, an Item 2.02 filing must include a copy of the earnings release. Letters provided by a former accountant must be filed as an exhibit to an Item 4.01 or 4.02 8-K, and a disgruntled director's letter must be filed as an exhibit to an Item 5.02 8-K. You also have to file copies of charter amendments under Item 5.03.

182. How do you know what exhibits need to accompany a filing?

There's a nifty chart in Item 601 of Regulation S-K that lists all of the various exhibit items and indicates which filings they're required to be included in.

183. How do you determine if a contract is "material"?

Unfortunately, you've got to use your judgment.

There are certain agreements in Item 1.01 that are presumed to not to be made in the ordinary course, and there's some guidance in Item 601 of S-K itself when it comes to the type of agreements that will trigger a filing requirement, but for the most part, you've got to assess "materiality" by reference to the Supreme Court's *Northway* and *Basic* "reasonable investor" standards.

184. If you file an exhibit once, do you need to keep incorporating it in future filings?

Yes, you're typically required to continue incorporating an exhibit in subsequent filings that call for it.

185. Can you omit schedules and exhibits to an acquisition agreement from the agreement that you file?

Yes. Item 601(b) (2) says that schedules (or similar attachments) shall not be filed unless they contain material information which is not otherwise disclosed in the agreement or the disclosure document.

Most people take the position that garden variety disclosure schedules are encompassed by this exclusion, but that side deals and other substantive provisions buried in schedules don't make the cut.

Schedules are only allowed to be excluded from acquisition agreements filed under Item 601(b)(2). Filers often attempt to apply this to material contracts filed under Item 601(b)(10), but the Corp Fin Staff has objected to that practice.

Companies are required to file a list briefly identifying the contents of all omitted schedules, together with an agreement to furnish supplementally a copy of any omitted schedule to the Corp Fin Staff upon request.

LL. Reporting Director & Executive Officer Transitions

186. When is a company required to file a Form 8-K in connection with the departure of a director or an executive officer?

Item 5.02 says that a company has an obligation to file an 8-K if the company's principal executive officer, president, principal financial officer, principal accounting officer, principal operating officer, or any person performing similar functions, or any named executive officer, retires, resigns or is terminated from that position, or if a director retires, resigns, is removed, or refuses to stand for re-election.

There's also a specific trigger for director resignations tied to disagreements on policies that requires more detailed disclosure.

We analyze a bunch of various scenarios in our "Director Resignation & Retirement Disclosure Handbook" posted on TheCorporateCounsel.net.

187. What information is required to be contained in that 8-K?

If there's no reportable disagreement in connection with a director's resignation, you merely have to disclose the fact that the separation event has occurred with respect to a director or executive officer and the date of the event. If any compensation arrangements are entered into or modified with an executive officer in connection with the departure, you need to disclose those as well.

If a director has resigned or refuses to stand for re-election because of a disagreement with the company, known to an executive officer, on any matter relating to the company's operations, policies or practices, or if a director has been removed for cause from the board of directors, then you have to disclose not just the fact of the resignation, but the reasons for it and any correspondence the director gave you.

You also have to show your disclosure to the director and file any response you get stating whether the person agrees or disagrees with it.

188. What is the triggering date for an 8-K relating to the retirement of an executive officer or director?

The 8-K is triggered by notice of the decision to resign or retire, not the actual departure or retirement of an executive or a director. At the same time, "discussions or considerations" of retirement or resignation do not trigger a filing obligation.

The SEC says that is a facts & circumstances issue - and it can create an odd kabuki where someone informs the board that they are "considering" resignation or retirement so as not to cross the line and trigger disclosure.

In order to avoid the grey areas that this kind of thing can create, some companies adopt resignation policies that provide for specific notice mechanisms to be complied with as part of any departure.

189. Will the appointment of a new director or executive officer require an 8-K?

Yes, if it's a new principal executive officer, president, principal financial officer or principal accounting officer.

You can defer the filing until you've made a public announcement of the new hire – but if you opt for this approach, the 8-K is due on the day of the announcement, not four business days later if you opt for this approach.

190. **What information is required in an 8-K reporting a new director or executive officer?**

For a new executive, companies have to disclose the biographical and five-year business history required under Item 401 of Reg S-K, as well as any family relationships with any other director or officer. Any related party transactions under Item 404 of Reg S-K have to be disclosed, and any compensation arrangements with the new executive need to be disclosed as well.

For a new director, the information requirements are more limited. In addition to identifying the individual, the company has to disclose what committees they will serve on and any related party transactions subject to disclosure under Item 404 of Reg S-K.

Any arrangements or understandings that resulted in the appointment have to be disclosed, and any compensation arrangements that were entered into or modified in connection with the director's appointment have to be disclosed.

Note that this 8-K requirement is only applicable to directors who are not elected by shareholders.

MM. Reporting Acquisitions & Divestitures

191. When are companies required to file a Form 8-K for an acquisition?

There are multiple potential triggers. Item 1.01 may trigger a filing because the acquisition involves a material definitive agreement. Item 2.01 will trigger a filing upon closing of a transaction involving a "significant" amount of assets. If the deal is sizeable, Item 9.01 may also require the disclosure of acquired company and pro forma financial information.

192. Will more than one 8-K filing be required for an acquisition?

Yes. A significant acquisition could trigger an Item1.01 8-K on signing, an Item 2.01 8-K on closing, and an amendment containing acquired company financial statements will be due within 71 days of the filing of the Item 2.01 8-K.

193. What triggers an obligation to file acquired company financial statements and pro formas?

It's the size of the business that's being acquired. If it is a "significant subsidiary" as defined in Rule 1-02 of S-X, and it meets the thresholds set forth in Rule 3-05 of S-X, then you'll need to have 1, 2 or 3 years of audited financial statements and unaudited interim statements – plus pro formas – in the 8-K.

A subsidiary is significant under S-X if:

1. The value of the investments in and advances to the subsidiary by the buyer exceed 10% of the value of the assets of the buyer's consolidated assets,
2. The target's total net income exceeds 10% of the buyer's, or
3. The target's total assets exceed 10% of the buyer's.

Now, if everything is just at the 10% level, you don't need financials. If any of the tests trips 20%, then you need a year of financials. If any of the tests trips 40%, you need 2 years, and if any of them trips 50%, you need 3 years.

194. Does the timing of the financial statement requirement depend on whether or not you're also doing a public offering of securities?

Yes. Because registration statements require any financial statements required by Rule 3-05 of S-X at the time of filing, and because 3-05 requires audited financial statements for acquisitions of significant subsidiaries that have been completed or are "probable," you may have to include acquired company financials in your registration statement (either in the document or by incorporating by reference to an 8-K).

There is a bright-line test that says you must include these in a registration statement for any acquisition that is significant at the 50% level. At lower levels, it depends on the offering participants' assessment of materiality.

In practice, some level of financial disclosure is frequently included in prospectuses relating to offerings in which the company has recently made a significant acquisition, even if audited numbers aren't required, although the level of that disclosure may vary.

195. What financial information must you file for a divestiture?

If you're divesting a significant business, you need to include pro forma financial statements giving effect to the transaction in your Form 8-K.

If the business that's being disposed of has not yet been reflected in reflected in the seller's historical statements as a discontinued operation, then you have to provide pro formas for the three years presented in the seller's most recent Form 10-K. Otherwise, a single year of pro forma information is required. Subsequent interim periods also need pro formas.

NN. SEC Comment Letters - Basics

196. How often are a company's filings with the SEC reviewed by the SEC Staff?

They're supposed to be reviewed at least once every three years under Sarbanes-Oxley, but some companies get reviewed much more frequently than others. I've worked with companies that get reviewed almost every year.

By the way, you may get reviewed on your Exchange Act reports and not know it – if the Corp Fin Staff doesn't have any comments, you'll never know that your filing was reviewed. You'll always know whether or not you're getting reviewed if you are filing a registration statement or proxy statement for a deal.

197. What is the Division of Corporation Finance (aka "Corp Fin")?

Corp Fin is the "Division" within the SEC charged with regulating disclosure made by public companies. Its responsible for reviewing public company filings and providing interpretive advice to companies and investors concerning compliance with the federal securities laws and SEC rules in their capital raising, reporting & M&A activities.

It is one of five Divisions at the SEC – the other four are: Enforcement, Investment Management, Trading & Markets and Economic & Risk Analysis.

198. How quickly will a company be required to respond to the Corp Fin Staff's comments? Can you get an extension?

For comments on your Exchange Act filings, the Corp Fin Staff will typically ask you to respond within 10 business days. Extensions are readily available (2 weeks is pretty standard), although some Staff members tell you that you need to request an extension in writing.

You're in control of the response deadline for comments on an offering, but if it sits around too long without a response, they'll ask what's going on and may ask if you're going to withdraw the registration statement.

199. What should you do if you don't understand or disagree with a comment?

Pick up the phone and call the examiner reviewing your filing if you don't understand a comment. Corp Fin is very willing to respond to questions. Don't waste everybody's time filing a response to a comment that you don't understand.

As for comments that you disagree with, that's what the comment process is for. If you think the Staff is wrong, tell them why in your response letter. That sometimes will persuade them. More often, it leads to further questions – but ultimately, things may go your way.

If you're unable to resolve things, then it's sometimes appropriate to schedule a call with the Staff. Sometimes, they may even reach out to you to do this – I had the accounting staff at Corp Fin reach out to one of my clients to request a conference call not too long ago to discuss its approach to segment reporting.

We spent about 30 minutes on the phone and were able to address the staff's concerns after going through a couple of unproductive rounds of comments.

If you're at loggerheads, and the issue is important enough to you, you can move up the chain of command and go over the reviewer's head. As a courtesy, I recommend that you tell your reviewer that you plan to do this.

The bottom line is the Staff's comments are often just that – and in some instances, they either don't understand your approach or are mistaken in their application of a disclosure requirement to your particular situation. Comments get addressed like this all the time.

200. How should you format a response letter?

You should reproduce each comment that you received and provide your answer below it. Many times, they explicitly request you to do this. It makes the process of reviewing your responses much easier – and you want to make it as easy on the Staff as possible for a quicker resolution of issues.

201. Who is typically responsible for responding to Corp Fin Staff comments?

It's typically a group effort, and who takes the lead on it varies. Typically, the company's lawyers will address the legal comments, while any comments on accounting or financial reporting issues are commonly addressed by the company's accounting staff.

Outside advisors, including outside counsel and the company's auditors, are usually involved as well. If the comments are solely accounting-related, the comment letter may be responded to by the company's CFO or CAO.

If the comments are broader, then I've typically seen the legal department – or outside counsel in smaller companies – take the lead in preparing the response letter, even if there are accounting comments as well.

OO. SEC Comment Letters – Timing

202. How do you know if your Form 10-K or proxy statement is likely to be reviewed?

The Corp Fin Staff has criteria that it uses to decide whether a particular filing will be reviewed, but these aren't made public. Nevertheless, you can make educated guesses.

First, you know that everybody is supposed to be reviewed at least once every three years, but if you have had significant developments in your business – major acquisitions, litigation, regulatory issues, substantial charges, unusual business transactions – or if you're an outlier in some fashion (e.g., perform better or worse than your peers, have key accounting policies that are different from others in your industry), you should can pretty much expect to receive a comment letter.

If you check any of these boxes and are a frequent capital markets issuer, then you're likely to be dealing with an almost annual event when it comes to Corp Fin Staff review.

203. Are there different levels of review that the Corp Fin Staff can undertake?

Yes. The Corp Fin Staff can opt to fully review a filing, or merely focus on a particular section or issue that interests them.

204. How long will it take for the SEC Staff to issue an initial comment letter?

Well, if we're talking about Exchange Act filings, it's really when they get around to it. Most of the time, when I've had clients get comments on their 10-K filings, it's usually been around the time of their annual meetings – maybe shortly thereafter. But they can come at any time.

It's different with Securities Act filings – if you get full review, they try to get you a comment letter on the initial filing within 30 days. If review is more limited, you may get a letter within a couple of weeks. Response times for subsequent filings on deals become progressively shorter.

205. How many amendments does it typically take to clear SEC Staff review?

It depends on the nature of the Corp Fin comments. If we're talking about an IPO comment letter with 75+ comments, you're going to be there awhile – it can frequently take 3 or 4 amendments to your document to clear comments.

Again, if you're a more seasoned company and you have the bad luck to get your deal pulled for review, it will likely take fewer turns to address the comments. On Exchange Act stuff, it usually takes a couple of back-and-forth's with the Staff to clear comments if they're fairly extensive. Sometimes, there may be one or two comments that require more time to resolve.

206. Do you have to satisfy the SEC Staff's comments before you can move forward with any deal you have pending?

That depends on the deal. If you need to register your shares and you don't have an effective registration statement, then you're going to have to satisfy the Staff because they hold the power over whether or not to declare you effective.

If you've got an effective shelf on file, then you can do a takedown without clearing comments on your 34 Act filings – but if you've got big comments that are unresolved, then you and your underwriters may want think hard about whether you want to move forward until they're resolved.

At the very least, you've got a disclosure issue – unresolved Staff comments are a line item that must be addressed. Large accelerated filers and accelerated filers are now required to disclose in their 10-Ks whether they have unresolved written Staff comments on their periodic or current reports issued more than 180 days before the end of the fiscal year.

These companies also must disclose the substance of any of the unresolved comments that they believe are material – and can include their position on the unresolved comments if they so desire.

If you're doing an acquisition, you can mail your proxy without clearing comments (assuming you've waited 10 days) – but that's guts ball. You may have to supplement your materials – and potentially delay your meeting - if the comments result in substantial changes.

If you're doing a tender offer, you don't wait for comments – you have to be ready to accept tenders from the moment you launch. Your tender offer filing goes to the top of the pile at Corp Fin and you'll get comments within a couple of weeks. Depending on their nature, you may have to amend your documents and, sometimes, extend the period for your tender offer.

PP. Rule 10b5-1 Plans

207. What are the benefits of a Rule 10b5-1 trading plan?

Historically, insiders have had a hard time trying to find the right time to be in the market for their company's stock. Most insider trading policies give them only a narrow window period to trade, and even then, there may often be concerns that they're tainted with inside information that hasn't yet been disclosed.

A properly implemented 10b5-1 plan can allow insiders to be in the market for shares during periods when they would otherwise be prohibited due to their possession of material non-public information.

Rule 10b5-1 provides an affirmative defense to a claim that an insider violated Rule 10b-5 by trading "on the basis of" MNPI ("material non-public information"). There are a lot of hoops to jump through - a 10b5-1 plan must be in writing, established in good faith and not as part of a plan or scheme to evade the prohibitions of Rule 10b5-1.

The plan must be adopted at a time when the person trading was not "aware" of MNPI, and its terms must specify the amount, price and date of the trades to be made under the plan (or include a formula or similar mechanism for determining the amount, price and date).

The person trading under the plan must not exercise any subsequent influence over how, when or whether to make trades under the plan; trades must be made pursuant to the plan; and trades cannot be offset by hedging transactions.

208. Do companies adopt these plans as well as insiders?

They do - and for the same reasons. Company 10b5-1 plans focus solely on purchases, while insiders' plans tend to focus more on sales of shares.

209. When is the best time to adopt a 10b5-1 plan?

During a trading window, and when there's nothing going on. It's critical that these plans are adopted at a time when people are not in possession of material non-public information.

In order to further insulate transactions under these plans, there's also usually some kind of cooling off period before transactions under the plan commence.

210. Should the adoption of a 10b5-1 plan by a company or senior executive be disclosed?

For companies, these are usually implemented in connection with the announcement of a buyback authorized by the board of directors. The fact that the company is in the market for its shares is material information, so that needs to be disclosed. The fact that the company will use a 10b5-1 plan should also be disclosed.

It's also considered a best practice to publicly announce a 10b5-1 plan adopted by insiders. Among other things, it helps show the SEC good faith in the establishment of a plan.

It also gives a heads up to the market as to the fact that insiders will be selling, which may help reduce questions when Form 4s start showing up. If there are awkwardly timed trades, it will give you something to point the media to in order to dampen down the inevitable wailing about insider trading.

211. What are the downsides of a 10b5-1 plan?

It can be difficult to amend or modify or terminate – altering plan transactions can raise issues of good faith. It can create complications if the company is doing a securities offering (Reg M) or a tender offer or other M&A activity – although plans can be and frequently are drafted to provide for suspensions during these periods.

However, even here, there's potential concern, because insiders often exercise a great deal of control over the timing of transactions and announcements of deals, which can raise issues about good faith.

It doesn't stop the media from calling out insider trading (sales by insiders are always a good headline). If your plan says sell, you're going to sell – the optics can be bad if you have fortuitously timed trades. It won't insulate you completely from insider trading liability – and the requirements of the rule must be followed to the letter in order to provide an affirmative defense.

Entry into a plan while you have material nonpublic information won't protect you. It can create logistical issues for Section 16 reporting compliance. If the insider is a large holder, it may put downward pressure on the stock price.

For that matter, announcement of the adoption of a plan may also result in the market misperceiving the insider's intentions and views about the company's prospects – which can put downward pressure on the stock regardless of the size of the individual's holdings.

QQ. Stock Buybacks

212. Why do companies repurchase their own stock?

Traditionally, buybacks were a way to fund equity compensation plans without diluting existing shareholders through new issuances. However, they've become increasingly popular over the years as a way to improve returns on equity to shareholders and as an alternative to dividends.

If a company has cash that it can't deploy effectively, it will often opt to do a buyback in lieu of paying a dividend. A buyback reduces the number of outstanding shares and increases returns on equity – something a dividend doesn't accomplish. A buyback is also something that allows each individual shareholder the opportunity to decide whether or not to participate.

Although companies soft-peddle this due to concerns about manipulating the market, a decision to engage in a significant repurchase program signals the market that the company believes that its stock is undervalued. But, like a dividend, it also signals the market that the company is not growing as fast as perhaps it once did.

Some investors believe that a buyback program may raise questions about the company's strategic direction. Others dislike it because it's financial engineering –

producing results through manipulating the balance sheet rather than by growing the business.

213. What alternatives are available for stock repurchases?

There are many ways in which a company can buy back its stock. First, there's the open market repurchase plan – usually structured to comply with the safe harbor provisions of Rule 10b-18 under the Exchange Act.

Rule 10b-18 limits the volume, the timing, the pricing and the manner in which repurchases are conducted on the open market. Companies announce their buyback program and disclose the maximum number of shares being sought, and then they disclose the number of shares repurchased in any particular quarter in their Form 10-Qs.

Companies sometimes also structure their open market repurchase programs to comply with Rule 10b5-1, in order to further insulate them from liability and preserve their ability to trade during periods when they would otherwise have to be out of the market.

Another alternative is a privately negotiated buyback from an investor who is looking to unload a bloc of stock. This is done outside of 10b-18, which isn't available for these transactions – although you can do a bloc trade on an exchange. There's not the price manipulation potential in face-to-face transactions – these are private and never hit the tape.

Companies that are looking to acquire a large number of shares in a short period of time have a couple of options. The more traditional one is an issuer tender offer. This involves preparing an offer to purchase and Schedule TO and filing it with the SEC.

The offer needs to be conducted in compliance with Rule 13e-4, which means among other things that it has to be open for at least 20 business days, it has to be open to all holders, the same price has to be paid for the shares, and there are required proration provisions and withdrawal rights.

Like other tender offers, this filing gets reviewed by the SEC and commented on, and you might have to supplement or even extend your offer depending on the comments you receive.

A more recent innovation for companies that want to acquire a large number of shares in a short period of time is the accelerated share repurchase plans—also known as "ASRs." These are fairly complicated and involve entering into a "forward" contract with a broker at the inception of the program.

At that time, the company typically makes an upfront payment to the broker—and the broker borrows the company's shares in the market from existing shareholders and delivers those shares to the company. The broker satisfies its obligation to return the borrowed shares by purchasing shares in the open market during a pre-agreed period of time.

214. Why do companies often structure buybacks to comply with Rule 10b-18?

Whenever a company is in the market for its own shares, there's always the potential for claims that the company is attempting to manipulate the price of its own stock.

Rule 10b-18 provides a company (and its affiliated purchasers) with a "safe harbor" from liability for manipulation under Sections 9(a)(2) of the Act and Rule 10b-5 under the Act solely by reason of the manner, timing, price, and volume of their repurchases when they repurchase the company's common stock in the market in accordance with the rule's manner, timing, price, and volume conditions

215. What are the potential downsides of a stock repurchase?

Stock repurchases aren't always viewed positively by investors. Sure, they juice your returns, but buying back stock also says that you can't figure out ways to deploy your capital in a manner that's going to produce attractive returns to investors.

Investors are also suspicious because buybacks can be a tool to juice results (like EPS) that may result in increased comp for executive officers under incentive compensation plans.

216. What disclosures are required in connection with a stock repurchase?

That's a good question with a number of different answers. First, always remember that if you're in the market for your stock, you have a continuing duty to speak – you have to disclose any material non-public information in your possession, even if you aren't otherwise required to disclose it in an Exchange Act report. The exception to that requirement is a 10b5-1 plan.

In addition, the fact that you are in the market for your shares is material information, so any open market repurchase plan should be disclosed, along with any material terms of the plan.

Companies also should announce that they are entering into an accelerated stock repurchase program and should disclose the number of shares, pricing mechanism and the final settlement date for the transaction.

Companies don't typically disclose privately negotiated purchases of shares until after those are completed, but those will be disclosed in the next Exchange Act report and - if sizeable - are frequently announced upon closing.

If you opt for the tender offer route, then you'll need to comply with the disclosure requirements in Schedule TO – you'll be preparing a formal disclosure document laying out, among other things, the terms of the offer, the reasons for the offer, pricing provisions, the duration of the offer and any material conditions to closing. This is typically accompanied by a press release.

10271428R00118

Made in the USA
Monee, IL
26 August 2019